MW00511034

A NEW SONG RISES UP!

SHARING STRUGGLES TOWARD SALVATION

CARIN JAYNE CASEY

KWE
PUBLISHING, LLC

Casey, Carin Jayne. *A New Song Rises Up! Sharing Struggles Toward Salvation.*

Copyright © 2020 by Carin Jayne Casey

Published by KWE Publishing: www.kwepub.com

ISBN (paperback): 978-1-950306-46-6 (ebook): 978-1-950306-47-3

Library of Congress Control Number: 2020913115

First Edition. All rights reserved. No portion of this book may be reproduced, stored in a retrieval system, or transmitted in any form or by any means — including by not limited to electronic, mechanical, digital, photocopy, recording, scanning, blogging or other — except for brief quotations in critical reviews, blogs, or articles, without the prior written permission of the author, Carin Jayne Casey.

Unless otherwise noted, scripture in this book taken from the Authorized King James Bible. (Published by the World Publishing Company, New York.) New International Version (NIV) Holy Bible, New International Version ® NIV ® Copyright © 1973, 1978, 1984, 2011 by Biblica, Inc. ® Used by permission. All rights reserved worldwide.

Casey, Carin Jayne: A New Song Rises Up! Sharing Struggles Toward Salvation

1. Christian Living - Social Issues 2. Christian Living - Inspirational 3. Body, Mind and Spirit - Healing - Prayers & Spiritual

NATIONAL DOMESTIC VIOLENCE HOTLINE

1-800-799-7233 or (TTY) 1-800-787-3224

CONTENTS

ACKNOWLEDGMENTS

To my husband, family, siblings, and close friends go my sincere appreciation for believing in me, and for continually proffering me with your patience, positive support, and understanding. Always, I felt the Lord's inspiration, guidance, and grace during this writing adventure; for that, I am profoundly grateful. As I approached completion of this adventure, the Lord inspired me into my next writing, *Stand With Your Armor On,* which I anticipate to publish in the Spring of 2021.

I am blessed with several awesome friends who are consistently supportive, whether in a business sense or spiritually; all encourage success within my calling. Those who immediately come to mind include: Vangie Hendrickson, Nayeli Cardona, Yolanda Gray, Angela B. Brown, Sharvette Mitchell, Tina Husk, Kamen Gordon, and Kristin Spiers. I sincerely appreciate each of you.

Specifically, I am grateful for the awesome kindness and support – especially patience, throughout my writings by my publisher and friend, Kim Wells Eley of KWE Publishing. And, many accolades for her expertise, generous guidance, and for pointing me to excellent resources, all to enable this story to come to life. I look forward to continuing our work together in future adventures.

INTRODUCTION

Can we agree that we live in uncertain times, full of unexpected trials and circumstances that are often overwhelming and excruciatingly painful?

If I could share with you a way for you to navigate through your challenges while at the same time enjoying peace, and not fear, would you be interested?

My desire is to help you to learn from the problems you face and to become empowered, content, and at peace along your journey. That desire for your deliverance was dropped into my spirit as I gratefully survived horrible and life-threatening experiences.

I came to realize that through my own dark days, there is ultimately light:

- I was not alone; the Lord was with me.
- Everything that happened, both good and bad, can be utilized as learning tools for my growth.
- As the Lord rescued me time after time my faith

increased, as well as a compassion for others in those same areas.

- It was because of my valuable learning through the hard times that enabled me to share the 'recipe to overcome,' which can be applied to any challenge in life.
- I know my unique purpose, what I was created for; as I serve the Lord and others within my calling, my life becomes complete.

This is my testimony: I was close to death in the pit of despair. But God heard my desperate cry. Now within me, I have a new song to sing, that of praise to my Awesome Deliverer.

What I want for every reader is positive, redemptive change. Regardless of any situation you may travel, my desire is for you to discover your secret for inner peace and joy.

PREFACE

While I was a young child, I remember asking an invisible God, "Why am I here?" Truly, I did not understand; I lived within a home of violence, confusion, and child abuse. As I attempted to protect younger siblings, I thought this must be the reason. As an adult, I wondered again why I existed while living in domestic violence and other abuses.

But the Lord was with me, bringing me up through all of the darkness I faced. Along the way I learned valuable lessons that I can share with others. I have been well educated regarding child abuse, domestic violence, and other abuses through the world of hard knocks.

When I rededicated my life to the Lord around seven years ago, my gratitude motivated me to help others to overcome the demons in their lives. Because of my own experiences, my initial interest has been in women coming from domestic violence. I wrote *My Dear Rosa Jean*, a fictional novel that depicts how easily a woman can be entrapped by an experienced abuser, her struggles through typical types of abuses that happen, her desperate quandary whether safety lies with staying or leaving, and her walk with the Lord into recovery.

Mystery at Candice Bay includes within the storyline struggles teenagers may face. My website, *www.CarinJayneCasey.com* also contains valuable information about domestic violence and references, as well as information about books that I have written.

I began to join in annual mission work with local church missions (Hope Point Church and Mechanicsville Christian Center) and other groups that converge in New York City at New York School of Urban Ministry. We are assigned street ministry the night of arrival. The next day we serve women at shelters with cosmetics, hair styles, massages, manicures, pedicures, clothes, jewelry, and plenty of prayer, love, and comforting words. The women resonate well with *My Dear Rosa Jean*. In the name of Jesus, we are His vessels of blessings to these women in need.

It has been a while since I wrote my first novel, and there is so much more I have learned and want to share so that my precious readers can benefit and find healing. Again, my deepest love is for women who have suffered or continue to suffer the effects of abuse. With help from the Lord and other people, the message within these pages will be shared with these women.

What do I share? I candidly share bits and pieces of my testimony with encouragement to those who may resonate. I provide experiences of various attacks initiated by the wickedness in this world. I provide what I have learned in each instance. Through it all we have ample scriptures available for study, support, and maturity.

This book, with its corresponding *A New Song Rises Up Study Guide*, is not an expose or memoire, so purposely there are no names of people included. Rather, this is geared to be helpful. It includes only the necessary pieces of my testimony to get the point across. Any testimony should always point to the love, power, healing, and justice of our Almighty God. My effort and hope is to encourage every reader to turn to God for forgiveness, rescue, and salvation through Jesus Christ so that they too can enjoy the inner joy and peace that is in me, regardless of the circumstances surrounding me.

1

PROLOGUE

I self-consciously sat alone at a secluded table in that dimly lit, sleazy bar, as I watched him intimately conversing with the other woman. She looked into his eyes earnestly as she begged him to make me leave, but he would not.

Apparently, she did not have enough experience with him, or she would have known he had carefully orchestrated this strange and awkward encounter. Like a cat playing with his mice, he thoroughly enjoyed my heartbreak, and her anxiety.

Meeting her in this way, without introductions from across the room, was particularly intimidating. Comparatively, she and I were opposites in appearance: different size, height, and race. He had told me her income and employment status, which was much higher up the ladder than mine. But what I saw before me was my equal, because she had allowed herself to be caught into the same malicious trap as I had.

I arrived with him after an entire day of abuse. The morning began with his decision I would meet a woman he was having an affair with. In the past he had insinuated there were others, but then denied it. I had chosen to believe he was not cheating on me, although he was often cruel with the threat of having affairs.

I had not been agreeable to his plan. Quickly, his horrid demands escalated to repetitive screaming and beating. Did it matter to him if being in her presence might destroy me? Exhausted and over-powered after a matter of hours, I had no choice but to obey his orders. I felt ugly and plain, not wearing makeup or an attractive outfit for the confrontation with my competitor. Without these options, I got into the car. Predictably, I felt the pain of humiliation even before the encounter was to happen.

While sitting and watching this very personal, disgusting soap opera rapidly unfolding from romantic to sexual overtones before me, I found my solitude for uninterrupted thoughts welcoming.

He had finally gone too far, after all I had allowed myself to suffer. I endured tortures, sorrows, and abuses I can never tell, plus estrangement from my children. All these horrors had happened during these several months, bringing me to this moment.

It had been the only piece left that kept me with him; I had believed our relationship was monogamous, that I was his one and only. I always mentally struggled to believe his claims of sexual loyalty. How foolish!

I wondered at my misplaced trust, historically existing regardless of the multiple abuses, and even following the time he had attempted to kill me. I always forgave, and I always stayed. Why? I stayed because he would apologize, explaining he had been out of control, that he loved me, and if only I hadn't caused his outbursts, it wouldn't have happened. I repeatedly convinced myself there was still hope.

But with this encounter, he had presented what I understood to be undeniable proof that his recent claims were true; he had other women in his life. They were not just casual relationships, either. I reluctantly admitted it while I witnessed this couple petting, touching, and loving on each other in such intimacy before me.

How could I find animosity toward her? She too was his victim. I could envision much pain and heartbreak in her future. I hoped she would survive. I hoped we both would. I needed to keep us both in prayer.

I knew my abuser meant for this to be the final blow of the sledgehammer upon my head, the final sharp stab running through my heart. It was meant to cause me insurmountable suffering. But instead, what worked inside me was not destruction, but the demise of our relationship. Within me was knowledge of finality to the hell I had been living in.

Yes, I calmly told myself, I have a new hope for life without him, without abuse and torment. And I remembered. How many times has the Lord told me this? What the enemy, my adversary, the devil, *this man* meant for my harm, my God can turn it for good, for *my* good.

With a renewed clarity, I could see the truth in all I had experienced with this demonically abusive man. Especially, I recalled the time he had tried to kill me.

He and I had just experienced our first Christmas together, with all his family surrounding us. What a joyful time we had together. But after they left, his demeanor suddenly became dark as he yelled for me to come sit in the living room with him.

What had I done to cause this sudden change in his attitude? Nothing.

I had become frightened that I would react with emotionally igniting words or expressions, and I was afraid it would trigger him to explode. As much as I had tried for the past several months, I was not able to hide my feelings when upset, which caused him to go off into a rage.

I quickly left to get an antidepressant before sitting with him. But while upstairs, I heard a loud noise from the living room. First, I thought something had fallen. But then, in terror, I realized that he had thrown the Christmas tree onto the floor, ornaments and all. He had already gone into a violent rampage.

Where was I? Trapped upstairs. "I froze... It was like slow motion, watching him lumber toward me through the only available doorway; it was sort of like when I was a child walking the train tracks and watching a locomotive meandering toward me."[1]

It was astounding how quickly circumstances changed.

At one moment, I was celebrating Christmas with a loving family; and within days I was welcoming in the New Year, thankful to have survived a near-death experience, while residing at a YWCA women's shelter for domestic violence abuse victims. Even then, "full of conviction to sever my relationship" with him, "as I looked at another woman's freshly slit eyelid," I hoped he wouldn't "think of doing that to me. At least subconsciously, I intended to forgive and reconcile."[2]

As I relooked at that horrific scene, I realized it was not a spontaneous attack due to an uncontrollable explosion of rage, as it had appeared. No, it had been carefully planned.

The "tell" was not in the bloody and vicious beatings I received from one room into another. The "tell" was not when he ripped my jewelry off my fingers in the bedroom, leaving bloody skin scraped off.

But when he threw me onto the bed, and rolled me onto my stomach, what did he do next? That was "telling."

He reached for a rope at the front bed post with one hand, while he pulled my right hand toward it. I was filled with terror that sodomy was to follow; I quickly flipped onto my back with my legs squeezed up into my chest. He then sat on me, dragging my legs down, and mounted his knee upon my throat. My air passage closed-up. I couldn't breathe at all.

Inside, I screamed, "Oh God! He's going to kill me!"

And then, he let up a little bit, enough for me to whisper, "I told."

Confused at what I had said, he moved and sat at the side of the bed. With careful wording, he inquired about what I just said, but I couldn't understand it myself. I didn't answer.

Because of those two short words that I didn't understand even uttering, I found opportunity to escape! The path, and the seconds were provided for me. Meanwhile, this malicious man quietly sat in deep concentration, while he remained confused.

I had always looked back on that scene as God stepping in to save me, and I know it was. With a renewed mindset, I finally came to see the full truth, the proof of the premeditation in that life-threatening incident. The rope was already there! The rope was a significant part of the plan for my suffering, and for my demise. What seemed to be a fit of rage had been calculated.

I had an epiphany.

"From my beginning, my Lord Jesus Christ traveled with me all along, through both horrible and wonderful adventures. He was always ensuring nothing is beyond what I can bear, and every situation provided ample choices. He was always with me, now on Earth, and forever after.

My very existence today is result of numerous lifetime miracles. It was Jesus who heard my lonely cry, brought caring people, usually strangers, into my life. My hope, faith and trust are in Him. My Lord will never betray or fail me. But people can and will; that is 'free will.'

I continually appreciate all God has brought into my life, each meant as a gift from Him. I accept that sometimes I move toward people God did not mean for me to associate with.

I accept even if within God's will, an imperfect partner can freely decide to respond to evil ways or worldly pressures or fall to other temptations to negate our lives together.

It is incomprehensible what pain it may cause, but God knows it's temporary....

I'll always praise God; always be thankful!"[3]

But that epiphany, although transforming, was only the first layer to a greater, more significant life-changing realization.

Before I had met my abuser, I had already placed myself in harm's way. After the previous failed relationship, I had quit going to church. Then, I quit singing, and reading the Word of God. Finally, and almost without notice, I had quit praying. I had placed myself in the lone position for consequence and disaster.

It's scary how corruption crept into me so insidiously.

I had turned my back on the Lord after all he had done for me, after He had carried me through horrendous child abuse and broken relationships. In my turning away from Him, I was telling my Heavenly Father that I didn't need His help, His love; I didn't need Him.

We have free will; we're not robots. We can choose to make terribly wrong decisions, and sometimes those decisions have lasting or deadly consequences.

Turning my back on the Lord had been my deepest, darkest fall into the pit. What if I had not turned back? What if I had died in the night, before having a chance to change it? If God had not stepped in with those life-saving words, what more danger, wickedness, and torment would I have allowed into my life?

I am forever thankful for His mercy, knowing I did not deserve it. The Lord heard my cry; and, like a shepherd with a lost sheep, the shepherd went out to save the one, and returned it to the fold, the Lord rescued me.

Out of gratitude I share my testimony with others, essentially saying, "Look at what an awesome God we have! He rescued me, and he can rescue others." In doing this, my desire is to influence other people, especially women who have fallen victim to abuse, as well as those who face hard challenges in life, so that they will allow my message of hope, faith, and love to resonate with them.

Regardless of the many bad choices I've made during my sinful lifetime, and regardless of the insignificance of my being, the Lord forgave me, He rescued me, and He saved me. If he did this for me, He can and will do it for others!

Without intent to lecture or preach down to anyone, I share bits and pieces of my story, always hoping to prompt my precious readers to consider the advice and lessons within. Of course, this writing is prayerfully inspired and always intended to point toward His glory.

Sharing these pages of innermost dark, ugly skeletons from my closet is worth it if any one of my readers can, in some way, find their way to walk from what has presented them with hopelessness and despair. The Lord has in store for each of us an awesome, ever-lasting victory.

As a newly converted or "Baby" Christian still operating within a long period of recovery from life-threatening abuses, I wrote the fictional novel, *My Dear Rosa Jean.* That was my way at the time to share a cautionary tale, which was strikingly like my own journey. My hope then was the same as it is to-date:

- To encourage and empower others who may find themselves caught up in overwhelming challenges and circumstances that seem beyond their control.
- To bring an awareness of the spiritual warfare that is happening all around us.
- To introduce the spiritual path toward everlasting wholeness and victory, offered by Jesus, our Lord and Savior.

The following scripture loosely describes my predicament in life; my plight seemed to be filled with fear, desperation, and hopelessness, lacking a sense of worthiness or belonging. But when I turned to the Lord, He mercifully changed all that. My life is a miracle, and I'm filled with gratitude.

With God holding me up, I can remain secure and grounded in faith, regardless of what this world may throw at me. I strive not to let my focus remain on my temporary stay on earth. A peaceful, joyful, and secure everlasting future with Him is ultimately what I want for myself, and for every person.

"He stooped down to lift me out of danger
from the desolate pit I was in,
out of the muddy mess I had fallen into.
Now He's lifted me up into a firm, secure place
and steadied me while I walk along His ascending path.
A new song for a new day rises up in me
every time I think about how He breaks through for me!
Ecstatic praise pours out of my mouth until
everyone hears how God has set me free.

CARIN JAYNE CASEY

Many will see His miracles;
they'll stand in awe of God and fall in love with Him!"
Psalm 40:2-3 TPT (The Passion Translation) (emphasis added)

2

ARE YOU BELIEVING THE LIES?

*M*y humble beginning was in a dysfunctional, sometimes violent home. My mother loved me for a moment, even treated me as her favorite, and then suddenly, she would be screaming hysterically while she beat me (with a brush, fists, or something else). What did I do to deserve this? My three-year old mind didn't understand. Always, my little sister watched this violent scene in terror. This pattern of child abuse was on-going.

I would wonder, why didn't my daddy come to save me? He was in the house, usually in the other room! Surely, he heard the scream-ing, and the hits. He could see the bruises. My explanation made sense: there was something about me that made me unlovable.

From this humble beginning, I sensed that I was unloved, not enough, unimportant. At least, that's what my parents' behavior taught me.

My first lesson was a lie, straight from the enemy in hell, but over time I felt that lesson to be continually supported, while teaching me most assuredly that there was something about me that caused me to be unlovable. This was the first of many lies, but it was the core lie which all others were built upon.

What were some of the other lies the enemy sought to impress on me? To name a few:

- You are not worthy.
- Your sins were so great that God will not forgive you.
- God has left you alone in this.
- What you do or don't do is of no importance to God.

I'm not speaking out of turn when I refer to the enemy of evil and darkness as a liar.

"'... He's been a murderer right from the start! He never stood with the One who is the true Prince, for he's full of nothing but lies— lying is his native tongue. He is a master of deception and the father of lies!'"
John 8:44 TPT (The Passion Translation)

Why would I believe such a lie, that I was not loveable?

As a child, I desperately tried to understand why I should suffer in such a dark world of chaotic dysfunction and cruelty. Why was I placed here, in this mess? What was the purpose in it?

Yes, I had experienced many crushing, debilitating struggles over the years. Some were life-threatening and harsh for longer than I could imagine enduring. Most every heartbreak throughout my life was because those who should have loved me, should have cared, were the very ones who seemingly sought out to destroy me.

And yet, here I am!

I had remained stuck in a mire of painful, debilitating lies about myself and about my worth for many years. Learning anything different was a timely work-in-process.

It may have taken a half-century (literally) to truly gain an understanding as to who I am, and why I'm here, and especially to learn that my life matters. I was enabled through the Lord's divine intervention to face the truth about myself, and therefore the chains that had held me down could be broken.

It was my sister who pointed out this truth to me a few years ago. After she had been desperately praying for her children, God revealed to her that if we can love our own without the Lord, and our Heavenly Father *is* love who loves us all, then we must realize that God loves our loved ones more than we do. It's amazing to realize that the Lord loves me even more than I love myself! I was no accident! Everything that happened to me was and is significant, and I have purpose.

You may feel that you've got it all together, your life is great, and you've never experienced any type of abuses or hardships with lasting effects.

Still, I may touch on something that needs resolution.

Have you pushed ugly stuff deep inside you? Maybe you were hoping that if you tamped it down far enough, it would never see the light of day, and it would never be in the open again.

But, do you realize that it's still there, affecting you in negative ways? When you haven't dealt with your heartbreak, suffering, and pain, then you're allowing it to fester and to morph into uglier stuff. But once it's brought to light, you can hope to recover, to overcome, and to enjoy the abundant life that was meant for you. You may not see it, but you did not come into being by accident or mistake. You were created deliberately!

"Before I formed you in the womb, I knew you..."
Jeremiah 1:5 NIV (New International Version)

You may believe that you are a mistake when compared to the lives of others. Maybe to you, they seem to have only minor issues. You see their lives as easier, more prosperous. Do you find anything positive in looking at others comparatively? Can you trade your life with anyone? And if so, do you truly know what that might entail? Do you think it's possible that they could have secrets and skeletons in their closet? And even if they have desirable talents, their skeletons may be so terrible that you would never want to trade?

I believe that we each are given a separate set of abilities and talents; and we each face different challenges. Maybe most of these challenges involve people-problems. I believe there is a spiritual struggle happening on planet earth. It's a battle ground between good and evil forces, both fighting for our souls. The evidence is when I hear of or witness crimes and malicious acts, experience offenses, and when I'm daily tempted to think, say, or do what I know is wrong.

I can say, I've learned far more in life through various challenges than during the periods of peace.

It's through hardships that I can see what I'm made of and the circumstances faced can be used as opportunity to mature. It's through the challenges I understand, or admit that I'm not self-sufficient, and I need the Lord to lean on.

I've learned that physical abuse is unfortunately just one of many tricks my adversaries may bring to me. Physical abuse is not measured as worse as or better than other abuses, in that nasty, evil bag of venom from hell.

Sometimes, when bad stuff happens, I wonder:

- Is it the evilness of this world affecting me?
- Is God allowing something to come along because it will eventually help me to mature?
- Could it be a small part in the bigger picture for good in the grand scheme of things?
- Am I being punished for my wrongdoings?

I noticed an interesting explanation for life happenings in the story of Joseph, the son of Jacob and Rachel, in the Old Testament. Joseph was hated by his jealous brothers so much that they had sold him into slavery, letting his father believe he was dead (Gen. 37:1-36). Years later, Joseph was assigned to be the master of all the grains in the land during a time of famine (Gen. 41:41). When reconciled with his brothers, he explained:

"You intended to harm me, but God intended it all for good."

Genesis 50:20 NLT (New Living Translation)

Although Joseph's life had seemed hard for many years, within those years he received favor. All that had happened in the life of Joseph, including the hard times, was intricate parts of God's larger, good plan.

Sometimes we receive various means of correction by our Heavenly Father. What good parent doesn't correct their child when they've gone astray? God is our Creator. He has the right to do what He may decide.

We've all experienced or witnessed it: good things can happen to bad people, and bad things can happen to good people on earth. Even while in the midst of bad stuff happening, whether for correction or by circumstance, we can rest in the knowledge that God is ultimately in control.

He is just. He is good. He is love.

I hope your story is different than mine. Maybe you didn't suffer physical abuses. But are there ugly explanations you've been telling yourself? Maybe they were because other people have mistreated or ignored you?

Do you have demons you've had to face?

Have you ever asked yourself these questions? If so, was it because you didn't know what your purpose was? Did you find, at that moment in time, that life just didn't make sense? Did you ever wonder if you were an accident?

Regardless of your pathway, I encourage you to take this walk with me. I believe my testimony can help you come to a renewal of your mindset about yourself, and about the Lord.

I remember asking into the air toward a divine force greater than me, before I knew anything about God, and before I began kindergarten, "Who am I, and why am I here?" I asked because life didn't make sense. I was born into a dysfunctional and volatile home, deep into child abuse that I could not escape.

I accepted Jesus Christ as my Savior while in my twenties, a young wife and mother. Unfortunately, I remained distracted with confusing and painful happenings of this world. I continued to flounder and failed at relationships.

While in my forties, I turned my back on God and lived a sinful life; I faced dire consequences. As I've shared earlier, while deep in a low point of despair, I cried out to the Lord, and He provided me a means of escape.

While in recovery, after God had brought me out of that life-threatening situation, I still wondered what my abilities and talents might be; and especially I wondered, what was my purpose in life?

Over time, I've come to believe that our Creator has specific plans for every person, and those plans were made even before conception.

"'For I know the plans I have for you,' says the LORD.
'They are plans for good and not for disaster,
to give you a future and a hope.'"
Jeremiah 29:11 NLT (New Living Translation)

The most defining moments (aka: traumatic periods) of my life produced the most valuable lessons learned. Nothing that happened was unimportant. King David said:

"You saw me before I was born. Every day of my life
was recorded in your book.
Every moment was laid out before a single day had passed."
Psalm 139:16 NLT (New Living Translation)

I want to emphasize that my past was used to mold me, equipping me to become more like Jesus. Throughout every moment, I can attest that God *used* what the enemy meant for my harm, and made it work for good. That's true for every person.

My life is a miracle!

In a dramatic, transforming way, I re-dedicated my life to Jesus about seven years ago. It required me to take a step of faith. That step was tremendous for me, because I lacked confidence in others.

I did not trust people, not even people in church, and especially not someone I loved.

For several years I was in a relationship with the church and with my significant other, yet I was not willing to commit. The Lord pressed me. Suddenly, I took that step of obedience; I joined the church and married my husband.

Immediately doors opened, and I finally could see the light along my path. I'm still traveling that journey and learning as I go. What was opened for me?

- God inspired me to write faith-based books.
- I began to work as a domestic violence advocate in missions and outreaches.
- As an Ambassador for Christ, I began presenting weekly faith-based podcasts.
- There are more adventures ahead!

If anyone had told me seven years ago that I would be an author, a podcaster, and work in the mission field, I wouldn't have believed them.

I wouldn't have realized what joy and fulfillment I would find in serving others. Always, I am filled with gratitude for all God has brought me through. That gratitude motivates me to share with others, in hopes of helping them to defeat the demons in their own lives, and to enjoy the abundant life Jesus had intended. I'm filled with excitement, knowing my message will resonate with readers.

"For we are God's masterpiece.
He has created us anew in Christ Jesus,
so we can do the good things He planned for us long ago."
Ephesians 2:10 NLT (New Living Translation)

Last year, while serving with a vast number of other volunteers from various churches, at the annual New York School of Urban

Ministry outreach to sheltered women, I surprised myself at what I said to the Lord.

I had finished praying with a precious woman following her tragic story of how she came to live on the streets of New York. We prayed for her rescue, healing, and salvation.

I heard myself thanking the Lord that I had my past experiences in abuse, so that I could relate with her, help her, and point her toward God's glory.

That's coming full circle! That's gaining an understanding.

"And we know that God causes everything to work together for the good of those who love God and are called according to his purpose for them."
Romans 8:28 NLT (New Living Translation)

If God can deliver me from the enemy's snares, He can do it for others. He can deliver you!

3

ARE YOU INVISIBLE?

*H*ave you ever felt like you were a part of a group, but then, when it was your turn to speak, no one acted as if you had said anything? You were being ignored. Worse, what if someone else began speaking over you, as if you weren't even talking? Did it feel as if you, your thoughts, your feelings did not matter? Were you invisible?

It hurts, doesn't it?

Do you feel as if you're the only person who has become invisible, although logic may say that it happens to others? Have you experienced such feelings as not belonging, or that you didn't matter, during your formative years, or as a teenager? Did you have someone to help you through it, or did you suffer alone and silently, letting those feelings go deep inside, and fester?

If you did experience childhood abuses of any kind, you may not have realized that the Lord cared about you, and there are people now who care about you. You may feel totally isolated and alone, but you are not.

Think about it. Do you find more or less confirmation throughout life that you don't matter, that it's okay for you to be mistreated, that you're not enough? If there's more of it poured on, it may be because you are conveying this belief to yourself, and to the world. By tamping it down without dealing with it, you may be falling into agreement with the enemy.

Jesus said:

"A thief has only one thing in mind—he wants to steal, slaughter, and destroy. But I have come to give you everything in abundance, more than you expect—life in its fullness until you overflow!"
John 10:10 TPT (The Passion Translation)

Why would I want to touch on such a sensitive topic that could be carefully buried into the past? I'm addressing the ugly stuff because the pain continues to be inside, festering and morphing into far worse matters to deal with; all that ugly stuff has been maneuvering into further ruination to lives.

I see it as choices we face daily. One choice is to decide to get needed help, with turning to the Lord as the top priority. In this choice is opportunity to become the best person, the best parent feasible, and to continue goodness throughout generations. There's opportunity to build a solid foundation for a healthy and loving legacy.

The alternate choice is one I may have entertained for a time, living in a pity-party, keeping a chip on my shoulder, feeling the world owed me something, and surviving with other negative outcomes. But that choice did not bring about an overcoming to challenges.

I am not a qualified counselor or minister, but I am qualified to speak about the gambit of abuses from my personal experience and studies. In fact, I recently made a rough count of the years I've wasted in relationships filled with one type of abuse or another. To my surprise, it was around seventy percent of my life to-date.

Seventy percent, that's terrible! But what would be worse than that?

• To lack learned lessons from past experiences.

- To continue in relationships where abuse exists.
- To withhold sharing my testimony with others about how the Lord scooped me out of my horrible pit.
- To be unable or unwilling to present the world with a better plan than a legacy of abuse.

Within child abuse, I was helpless, and truly unable to escape. But what about the domestic violence and other abuses that followed me throughout adulthood?

I may have remained in prison, but what I was unaware of is this: I was holding the key to that prison door. At any point, I could have turned to the Lord, and walked out of my prison of abuse.

I'll briefly share with you some of the basic abuses that a child may suffer. Some abuses I may describe are commonly known, like physical or verbal abuse. But there will be other instances that are not commonly associated with child abuse. When packaged together, the effects are compelling.

As I mentioned before, my mother physically abused me. She would be loving one moment, and suddenly go into a rage, and hysterically beat me. I had no way to prevent it or to control it; her beatings were not based upon how good or bad a child I was. So even while I enjoyed it when she decided to be affectionate, I continually waited for the other shoe to drop. The injuries were compounded with the sense of helplessness and fear.

Betrayal happened just as frequently, because my father never came to my rescue. He failed to protect his child repeatedly. Experience told me that parents who decide to do nothing when their child is in danger instead of nurturing, guarding and protecting their child can cause the most lasting pain of all.

By not coming to my rescue, my father was essentially telling me that I didn't matter, that I was invisible. What does a child tell themselves when their parents fail them? They do tell themselves *something* to explain the situation, and that explanation is usually negative toward themselves; thus, an acceptance is formed toward their lack of worth.

In my instance, such betrayal also brought on my resentment and anger toward my father. While I was a teenager, we had many conflicts, sometimes even terrible physical fights.

We're supposed to honor our parents, aren't we? That negative relationship continued until I had turned to the Lord while a young adult and mother. I'm so thankful that I was eventually able to forgive my father and we had a friendly relationship before his passing.

In scriptures we learn that when our father and mother forsake us, essentially abandoning us, then our Heavenly Father adopts us. This is why I survived the child abuse.

What about favoritism?

I grew up watching my father affectionately cooing and loving over my sister, who was only one and a half years younger, and I wondered, why not me? Am I invisible?

When I was five years old, I remember timidly approaching my mother while she ironed clothes. It took everything in me to do it, but I had to ask the hard question: "How come my daddy doesn't love me?"

She stopped ironing, and without looking at me, she began to cry. That was a portion of the answer I had hoped not to receive. But from that point on, I knew; my daddy didn't love me. It was heartbreaking, but I accepted it.

Favoritism went a bit further, to the point my parents seemingly pitted my sister and I against each other. My mother loved me (although she beat me), and my father loved my sister.

At any moment, either of them could shout hard statements against the child they did not favor. I'm amazed as I tell this that she and I were not 'arch-enemies,' rivaling throughout life. We were not. She and I remained as best friends growing up.

Regarding the harmful and lasting effects of favoritism, I've found comfort and understanding as I read in Genesis about the deceit, conflicts, jealousy, and heartaches caused within Abraham's family. I share some about their story in hopes it may also resonate with others regarding jealousy within the family.

Abraham's son, Isaac, born of Sarah, was favored over the oldest son, Ishmael, born of Sarah's Egyptian handmaiden, Hagar. That caused great strife between these sons and their families throughout history.

Isaac and his wife Rebekah each chose their favorite between their twins. Isaac favored Esau, while his wife favored Jacob (also known as Israel). You may recall I had mentioned Jacob's family in a previous chapter. Esau was the oldest, entitled to the birthright, but because of deceit by his mother and brother, he was cheated out of his inheritance and his father's blessing.

Fearing Esau's revenge, Jacob left their family home (Gen. 25:24-28:5). Rebekah lost out on spending time with her favored son.

Laban, a relative of Abraham, became Jacob's father in-law. By Laban's deceit Jacob was tricked into marriage with the older daughter, Leah, while he had meant to marry the love of his life, beautiful Rachel. Jealously and heartache flowed freely in that household. Rachel was loved, but she had no children. Leah was not loved, but was very fertile, and had many children (Gen. 29:23-35).

With each son she had for Jacob, Leah hoped he would admire and love her, and Rachel felt the sting of disgrace (Gen. 30:23 NIV). By the time Rachel finally had sons for Jacob, he already had six sons and a daughter by Leah, two sons by Rachel's handmaiden, and two sons by Leah's handmaiden. Rachel's first son was Joseph; she died when she gave birth to her second son, Benjamin.

Did the legacy of favoritism continue? Yes! Jacob favored Joseph and Benjamin over all the others because he had them in his old age (and they were born of Rachel). He made it obvious with special gifts, like the coat of many colors for only Joseph (Gen. 37:3 KJV).

When Jacob feared danger with his brother approaching the camp, he devised layers of protection for his family, with the priority in accordance with those he favored most. Who he favored among his children could not have been more obvious to his family (Gen. 33:1-3 ESV).

Certainly, I could relate to the insidious progression of pain and suffering that was caused in Abraham's family because of favoritism. With this biblical story, I could not tell if the persons showing favoritism had any idea they caused harm. Maybe they were oblivious to the evilness it carried, and to the chaotic pain that it caused. Regardless, I believe the intent of the enemy, the devil was evident.

"Be well balanced and always alert, because your enemy, the devil,
roams around incessantly, like a roaring lion
looking for its prey to devour."
1 Peter 5:8 TPT (The Passion Translation)

Somehow, knowing that even great people in biblical times experienced similar weaknesses within a dysfunctional family, I found a measure of peace about it. Favoritism is evil, but I couldn't label my father or mother as evil for their part in it. Happily, I can say that unlike Abraham's family, I don't see where anyone in my family continued the legacy of favoritism to the next generations. For that, I am thankful.

To this day, I'm sure many parents do favor one child over another. In a perfect world, the children will never realize it. Because of how it works negativity in the hearts and minds of the children, I believe it's vital for parents to care about each child's welfare, happiness, and even the smallest accomplishments.

I've found that the pain of verbal abuse can be debilitating. The view may be to minimize the abuse if it's verbal, as opposed to physical. As a person who has experienced both, I can attest (again) to this: One cannot adequately measure the severity of the pain, nor the lasting effects of one type of abuse against another. It's all bad.

Both of my parents could slice a person with their words. Accusations came from one, and insults from the other. To this day I'm sensitive to hearing anyone being called stupid or for such an implication to be made.

In evaluating the past, I considered how a person might feel about themselves following a childhood riddled with abuses mentioned here.

- Will they be less likely to come into adulthood with confidence and high self-esteem?
- Will they tend to view themselves as not enough, unworthy, and unloved?
- How will their emotions run? Angry, bitter, depressed, or sad?
- Will they lack trust in others?
- Might they pattern their behavior after those who have been abusive to them?
- Because of the various levels of dissociation in their past, might they find themselves unable to adequately express their emotions?

I surmised that the above feelings, beliefs, and resulting behaviors can affect the normal cycles of relationships in an adult life. It did with mine, until I became aware of it and decided to change my outlook and attitude.

As I look at some relationship cycles, these are some things I noticed:

- How likely is a person to seek higher education if they lack self-esteem, and think of themselves as stupid?

I wouldn't have attempted college had it not been for my husband (now deceased) insisting that I do it. I remember, as my successes and grades improved, my confidence grew.

- How likely would such a person go after that promotion at work, or to run their own business, if they have no confidence? Not very likely. A safe, lower position might appear more attractive.
- Will they know how to manage healthy relationships with friends, family, and their intimate partner? Do they even know what a healthy relationship entails? It's hard to fake something you don't have a clue about doing.

- With their abusive parents as the model from the beginning, how will a person likely view God? Will they view him as an unpredictable mixture of love and brutality? Will they see themselves as invisible to their Creator?
- Will they view God as authoritarian to the point they do the maximum good works and rituals of prayers in hopes for him to dole out his love in their direction? Will they become a workaholic, with no sense of satisfaction?
- Will they be less likely to love, trust, and rely upon the Lord in faith? Would they automatically feel rejected by him, and thus never turn to him at all? Because they don't feel worthy for God's love, they may angrily reject Him.

While in deep reflection of my history, I considered, what can a person do to bring about a lifetime of happiness, love, peace, and the sense of belonging?

I've put together what I call a recipe to overcome. And it literally can be applied to a multitude of challenges we may experience in life. Here, I'll explain the recipe to overcome, one ingredient at a time:

1. TURN TO GOD

Yes, this is the first step. Decide to turn your life around as I did while in the pit of despair. Humbly come to the Creator of the Universe, in prayer. Why? Because He created us, and He loves us, even more than we could possibly love ourselves. This is the most important thing you'll ever do, confess to Him, out loud!

"For God so loved the world that he gave his one and only Son, that whoever believes in him shall not perish but have eternal life."
John 3:16 NIV (New International Version)

Jesus, who knew no sin, came to earth to suffer and die on the cross, to pay for our sins. And He defeated death. Jesus Himself tells us:

> "'I am the way and the truth and the life. No one comes to the Father except through me.'"
> John 14:6 NIV (New International Version)

We can humbly come to the Lord ourselves. We can pray to Him directly for forgiveness, rescue, and for salvation. When we accept Jesus as our Lord and Savior, we have begun our relationship with Him.

We were not made to be robots, so we don't automatically worship the Lord. No, He gave us free will to make that decision to turn to Him or not. We don't need to be a great scholar to understand the way to the Lord, and to have eternal life with Him. There are many supporting scriptures, such as Romans 10:9-10 and 1 John 1:9 that share the salvation message, but these two verses (John 3:16 and John 14:6), above, spell it out plainly.

2. SAFELY LEAVE YOUR DANGEROUS ENVIRONMENT

If anyone is in an abusive situation now, this step is very dangerous *and* necessary. That's why there are experts available to help individuals get out safely; they can help devise an escape plan.

If it's an emergency, dial "911."

If you find yourself in a domestic violence situation, there is much literature and resources available to support you; therefore, you are not alone and help is obtainable. The National Domestic Violence Hotline number is 1-800- 799- 7233 (SAFE).

Please know the Lord did not mean for you to remain in a habitually toxic environment with mean-spirited people. When you study Proverbs 22:24 and 1 Corinthians 5:11, you will see that the Lord doesn't want you to associate with those having a hot-temper or living a sinful lifestyle.

If a person's situation is not termed as physical abuse, and it's not domestic violence with an intimate partner either, is it abuse? Each person must examine their situation, asking: am I wasting time while allowing harm to myself, in a relationship with people who are habitually mean-spirited, manipulative, and malicious? This describes a toxic environment.

You might say, "I have to stay in it, it's my _____." (Fill in the blank: sister, church member, in-laws, boss, etc.)

But it doesn't matter who that habitually mean-spirited and malicious person is. They have caused their presence around you to become a toxic environment! In my opinion, nobody should remain in the constant presence with toxic people. Rather, the Lord wants each of us around people who build us up, people who will encourage us, who are loving, kind, generous, and speak lovely, pleasant, uplifting things.

3. HAVE FAITH AND BELIEVE

Have you turned to Jesus for your salvation? Then you need to realize you are not an unloved, unworthy abuse victim. You are not alone. Rather, you are a precious child of God. The King of the Universe loves you, and you are never without His presence.

Have faith, not fear. We have the choice whether to live a life of fear, or of faith. We can only choose one. When we believe and accept Jesus, our mind is renewed. I encourage you to study Jeremiah 31:3 and Isaiah 41:10, where God shares assurance of His love and devotion. In short, this is my testimony:

Without Jesus, I saw myself as unloved, unworthy,
not enough, and an abuse victim.
With Jesus: I am loved. I am worthy. I am enough.
I am a child of God!
I *am* a daughter of the Most High King!

4. GRATITUDE

Look with thanksgiving at what the Lord has done for you, what storms He has brought you through. When we rejoice in the Lord, praising Him, we can experience inner peace and joy despite our circumstances. We can look at all that the Lord has done for us, how He has rescued us, and be thankful for every breath we take.

Rather than look back at the past with self-pity, we can walk in the present moment and into the future with hope and gratitude. It's a choice we make. In Philippians 4:4 and 1 Thessalonians 5:16-18, we're encouraged to rejoice in the Lord always.

Some years ago, I whined and complained to a friend about unfair things that had happened. My friend patiently listened while I continued my pity-party. Thoughtfully, he suggested, "Hmm. It seems like you're just not thankful enough." I was taken aback with his statement; but he was right and to the point.

It's impossible to have a pity-party while being thankful.

5. FORGIVENESS

We forgive ourselves, the abusers in our lives, and we forgive those who remained indifferent to our need for help. We forgive for our own soul's sake.

Forgive yourself. Have you turned to Jesus? When you humbly asked forgiveness, He forgave you and your past is gone. Now you need to forgive yourself and forget the past.

Forgive those who abused or offended you. Forgive so your Heavenly Father will also forgive you. This happens in your heart and it may be dangerous to tell them. Regardless, forgiveness is not at all the same as trust. You may forgive, but maybe circumstances will indicate that you should never trust them again.

If trust comes, it should be over a matter of months, not days, after continual proof (without interruptions or irregularities) that the abusive person has become trustworthy.

Forgive the indifferent. Forgive those who knew of your

desperate need but chose to do nothing to help. We don't know what their reasons were; we don't know their heart.

I like to describe a hypothetical situation that I heard of years ago, to point out the difference in forgiveness versus trust. I do this because of my own experience of going back to a life-threatening domestic violence situation after I had forgiven my abuser, and it was only by the Lord's grace that I had the means to escape. Statistics tell us that victims of domestic violence all too often do go back to their abusers after they've forgiven them.

Here is the hypothetical situation: Imagine that you're in a boat with your abuser, and you're out into the middle of a lake. Then, your abuser tries to drown you. Somehow you manage to get back to shore, and you forgive them for what they've done.

Does that mean that you must go back into the boat, out into the middle of the lake again, with your abuser? Of course not!

To sum it up, a great way for you to prevent the continuation of abuse into generations to come would be to do everything you can to ensure that you are the most well-balanced, and healthy person you can be. That begins with turning to the Lord for help.

He can take your pain from the past, and give you inner peace and joy, regardless of what you may face. In 1 Peter 5:7 is encouragement to cast your cares on the Lord. Matthew 6: 14-15 reveals how important it is to forgive so that God will also forgive you.

By following the steps in my recipe to overcome, you are well on your way to bringing forward a legacy for wholesome, loving people.

4

WILL THE OFFENSES STOP?

*Y*ou might be thinking, "I've survived horrible abuse! But even now, people continue to treat me with meanness; they attack me, offend me, and try to abuse or use me. Will this pattern of offense ever stop? If so, when?"

I've shared with you some of the troubles of my own life. From this, I've developed a few thoughts about why the pattern of offense continued to happen. Allow me to share...

I believed the enemy when he told me that I wasn't good enough, that I was unworthy, and that there was something about me that made me unlovable. And I operated on that belief. It wasn't something I did consciously; there was no knowledgeable decision on my part, to present myself to the world as a rug for people to wipe their feet on. But there I was: a naïve, vulnerable little rug.

A person is relatively helpless while a child; they are dependent upon the parents or guardians in charge of caring for them. With that in mind, I was not able to change where I lived or with whom, not in my own power. After childhood, I had opportunity to change my environment, and to change my belief in myself. But my first intimate partner relationship was with someone who also came from a broken home, and we failed at keeping it together. My next opportunity for a solid relationship seemed promising, but while I was still a young adult, he suddenly died.

Life continues to happen around us; we need to seriously grasp hold of the good things and learn how to purposely let the bad stuff fall behind. At the same time, we need to strive to find the lessons meant for us to learn as we travel through life.

Following my husband's death, there were periods of promiscuity in my timeline. That may surprise some people, but it shouldn't.

When a person believes little about themselves, lacks a firm spiritual foundation, and has developed a pattern of accepting abuses or offenses, then bad stuff can happen within a sinful lifestyle.

I was needy and reckless, available for others to use and abuse this naïve, vulnerable little rug.

During that timeframe, I thought I had a target drawn on my back, because I seemed to attract people, especially men, who seemed to only want to use and abuse me. But as I studied it more closely (afterward, with twenty/twenty hindsight), I realized that wasn't the case.

I can recall there were many opportunities that came along for me to spend time with kind and loving people, but I had felt I wasn't good enough, and I was too far from belonging in their circle. I didn't see myself worthy of joining this group, or attending that church, or to date this nice man. I judged myself unworthy before they had opportunity to know me.

I invite you to ask yourself these questions. It will only take a moment for an insightful self-evaluation. Please decide:

- Am I needy?
- Am I reckless in the choices I make?
- Have I allowed myself to become a rug to others?

If your answer is yes to any of these, what can you do? Without any change on your part, will the offenses ever stop?

The easy thing to do is to tell yourself that you got to where you are *honestly*. The abuses and offenses you've received were not your fault, so you can't help being where you're at now. You're a true victim; it was just bad luck handed down to you. How does that resonate?

You can say that, but what good is there in such a thought process? It's a negative statement to say: "I'm a victim, I can't help it, I can't do anything about it." It may generate pity from some folks, but will that banner get you to a better place in life? No, it won't.

Or, you can be ashamed of yourself for the position you've found yourself in, and mentally beat yourself up every time you see where you've allowed another person to use and abuse you. While your offender is doing well, you're busy having negative self-talk in your free time. While your offender is having a good night's sleep, you're wide awake, hating them, and hating yourself.

Imagine this process of negative self-talk, mental self-belittling, and sleepless nights of emotion going on for decades without change. Does that make sense? You're essentially joining with the enemy to destroy you!

Am I saying I have no remorse for the things I've done in my past, including the promiscuity?

No. I had tremendous remorse for a very long time, and I sufficiently entertained and participated in self-hatred practices. In addition to the lack of self-esteem, there was much shame. Because of my low view of myself, I remained stuck.

I walked down the church aisle several times in humble repentance for my sinful living. Until one day the Lord helped me to realize this: He's not deaf.

He heard me the first time I came to Him! When I turned to the Lord for forgiveness, He could see what was in my heart, and He forgave me. In that moment of repentance, my Heavenly Father forgave me. I had to also forgive myself to see it.

My listing of past sins (regardless of how extensive that list may have been) is now gone. The Lord has now forgotten that list, so why should I revisit the shame of it, or attempt to remind Him of it? I shouldn't, the past is gone!

Does it matter what other people think? Do their opinions matter?

To a certain extent, everyone would want others to think the best, but I've found the efforts it may take to get others to form a good opinion can be exhausting.

If I've done something wrong in the past, and a person is aware of it, it will be remembered. Possibly, it will be thrown up into my face when I least expect it; and sadly, I may continue to be judged indefinitely.

But in the long run, after receiving the Lord's mercy, and having been gracious to myself in forgiveness, I can only do my best in life, and let the chips fall where they may. If another person wants to continue negative opinions or judge me, that's their choice. What would be a mistake on my part would be to 1) become a people-pleaser; or 2) let their opinion bring my own sense of self-worth down as well.

At the same time, I realize, haven't I done it myself at one time or another? Haven't I thoughtlessly criticized or judged another person, maybe even talked about them with others? Maybe I didn't view expressing an opinion as harmful, as gossip or slander. But was it?

Did I have all the facts before me? How could I know if I have the whole truth about anyone? Isn't it important to have the whole truth in order to form a solid opinion? Logically then, only the Lord is qualified to preside as judge, because He *is* the only one to know the whole truth (of course, this is an entirely separate line of thought to our country's judicial and legal systems, which I recognize as necessary).

Why would I set my happiness on what a mere person may think; with their thoughts changing as the wind blows? It's obviously nice when people are kind, but people will always be tempted with evil thoughts to harm each other in their words or actions. I can't depend on the opinions of others for my happiness. I concur that it's better to put my trust in the Lord, than to place my confidence in people. It's a matter of focus. My hope for restoration is in the Lord, my Creator.

One time while feeling broken down by the weight of judgment, I read this scripture and found comfort. What the Lord said to Israel, He says to you and me; His love is constant. His love is consistent.

"Long ago the LORD said to Israel:
'I have loved you, my people, with an everlasting love.
With unfailing love I have drawn you to myself.
I will rebuild you, my virgin Israel.
You will again be happy and dance merrily
with your tambourines.'"
Jeremiah 31:3-4 NLT (New Living Translation)

I'm no longer a rug! I can love myself and know the Lord loves me. But, will the offenses stop?

As I learned in church, the planet earth has suffered as a result of the fall ever since Adam and Eve gave in to evil temptation in the Garden of Eden. It's obvious that life on earth is temporary; living things each have their season that comes to an end. Even our treasures are in stages of rot and decay, rust and ruin.

As Jesus told us in scriptures, there will be challenges (trials, circumstances, situations with unsavory people) for us to face. Dealing with abuse and offenses is only part of our life challenges. We witness and experience crimes, floods, earthquakes, illnesses, disabilities, and wars, much of which we have no control over. So then, the answer to our question must be that offenses will still happen. Because of Jesus, we have hope; He shared with us the rest of the story. Jesus said:

"'And everything I've taught you is so that the peace which is in me will be in you and will give you great confidence as you rest in me. For in this unbelieving world you will experience trouble and sorrows, but you must

> be courageous,
> for I have conquered the world!'"
> John 16:33 TPT (The Passion Translation)

Daily we continue to face challenges. We experience spiritual warfare (good vs. evil), whether we choose to acknowledge it or not. But in the Bible passage we just read, we learn that Jesus has already overcome! When we believe and accept Jesus, in faith, we can hope for an eternity in heaven.

During our challenges on earth, we don't have to face them alone. We can pray, knowing the Lord is our strength and refuge, a very present help in times of trouble. As we patiently wait on the Lord, we can surround ourselves with people who are kind and loving, and experience inner peace and joy, even while we're still living in our struggles.

We can cast our cares on the Lord, knowing that He cares for us. When we do this, we can leave those people-problems with Him. He will handle them in His timing, and in His perfect will.

It may not look at all like we thought it might. Always know that God is well able to handle any situation we give to Him. Our job is to forgive, let it go, and walk away, in patient faith. We'll talk more about walking away from a toxic environment in the next chapter.

> "So here's what I've learned through it all:
> Leave all your cares and anxieties at the feet of the Lord,
> and measureless grace will strengthen you."
> Psalm 55:22 TPT (The Passion Translation)

I like to look at the Apostle Paul as an example for my life. He started his life out as Saul, a zealous persecutor of Christians. The Lord came to him, and Saul saw the light, he changed. Renamed Paul, he dedicated his life to Jesus.

Saul zealously killed people who loved the Lord; and yet, he was forgiven by his Creator. In fact, he was given a high calling as the Apostle Paul. He shared the salvation message and converted people into believers, worked with believers in the church toward maturity, and his good works pointed toward the glory of God.

If God forgave Saul, a murderer of Christians, then God can forgive me when I humbly repent of my sins. If God can forgive me, He can forgive you.

The Apostle Paul converted, and then became zealous for the Lord. Even while in prison and living in degraded conditions, he continued to preach the good news, content with inner peace in the Lord. He spoke of learning to be satisfied, or content, regardless of what conditions his environment was at the time. He was even content while in prison and preached to fellow prisoners and the guards. What was his secret?

There is something extraordinary that happens when a believer sets himself to praise the Lord, and remains thankful, regardless of his circumstances. The Apostle Paul encourages us:

"Let joy be your continual feast. Make your life a prayer. And in the midst of everything be always giving thanks, for this is God's perfect plan for you in Christ Jesus."
1 Thessalonians 5:16-18 TPT (The Passion Translation)

While in the midst of tremendous trial, we can put the chaos on pause to experience the present moment in prayer and rejoicing in the Lord. We can be thankful for the storms that are now past; we praise him for an anticipated good outcome in the future. We can sing songs and dance in praise, recite scriptures that demonstrate gratitude, and worship of the Lord.

So, you may ask, "Will the offenses stop?" To minimize the offenses that are lodged against you by specific adversaries of yours, you could seriously consider the second prong of the recipe to overcome; namely, to safely leave that dangerous or toxic environment. But having done that, can you expect or anticipate that all other people you encounter will treat you with love, kindness and respect? You already know the answer; not while your residence is on earth. But there is One who you can call upon for protection. Here is an example of such a prayer:

"O God, hear my prayer. Listen to my heart's cry.
For no matter where I am,
even when I'm far from home, I will cry out to You for a father's help. When I'm feeble and overwhelmed by life, guide me into Your glory, where I am safe and sheltered.
Lord, You are a paradise of protection to me. You lift me high above the fray. None of my foes can touch me when I'm held firmly in Your wrap-around presence! Keep me in this glory.
Let me live continually under Your splendor-shadow,
hiding my life in You forever."
Psalm 61:1-4 TPT (The Passion Translation) (emphasis added)

There will be times when the offenses don't stop or circumstances don't change; at least, not quickly. But we can change our focus to be on the Lord, and not on our problems. While we are rejoicing in the Lord, we're not worrying about anything. We're prayerfully thankful, with our hearts guarded. Guess what happens? Like the Apostle Paul who rejoiced while in prison, we are filled with inner joy and peace, regardless of our present circumstances.

Paul has written many books we read today in the New Testament. In these, he gives words of encouragement to believers, and stresses the importance of continual prayer and gratitude.

Regarding how we focus our thoughts, the Apostle Paul advises us...

"... Fix your thoughts on what is true, and honorable, and right, and pure, and lovely, and admirable. Think about things that are excellent and worthy of praise. Keep putting into practice all you learned and received from me—everything you heard from me and saw me doing. Then the God of peace will be with you."
Philippians 4:8-9 NLT (New Living Translation)

5

WHAT CAN YOU DO ABOUT TOXIC PEOPLE?

*I*n our relationships, do we know who is toxic? We may only make a mental note that we're uncomfortable, confused, and nervous when we spend any length of time with certain people. We may have lingering stress and irritation once we've walked away from them. Who among us, in our circle of relationships, is a habitually toxic person?

Toxicity in those you surround yourself with is a tremendously serious matter. Why? Because a toxic person can negatively affect how you view yourself and bring havoc to your own balance of emotions and morals. Your view of others may also become skewed. Realize that the toxicity of a person may come to you slowly and over a period of time, especially when they wear the disguise as your loved one or friend. Depending on who they are within your circle, you may believe you can do nothing about their negativity, igniting the feeling of being trapped.

I sincerely believe that a toxic person can bring to your life just as much destruction as child abuse or domestic violence. But your ability to recognize that you're in a toxic environment and that you can get out of it may not be as plainly obvious to you.

Initially, I thought I would ask you a series of questions to help you to determine whether there are one or more people within your circle of relationships who is repeatedly toxic to you. Instead, I want to give you a scenario to consider. If anything in this scenario reminds you of a specific person or persons, please think seriously whether you can afford to continue to have them as part of your circle of relationships.

Here is the scenario: Picture yourself entering the scene with a group of fellow women, your co-workers, relatives, friends or church members. You are glad to see them, and eager to converse with each of them. But then, Ms. Toxic is there, too. From experience, you have an idea of what to expect. Your feelings are complex: you are a good and loving person who wants to give everyone the benefit of a doubt, and you are filled with hope that they will change. But you feel yourself becoming agitated as your self-confidence falters. With dread in your heart, you hear yourself pray silently for the Lord to help you get through what ugliness may come.

While the women talk, it has come to your turn to share what you have been doing lately, and you are eager and excited to share information with your friends. Ms. Toxic interrupts within the first few seconds with a judgmental question, a sarcastic side remark, or to tell something important (which she believes is more important than what you have to say) that she had just remembered. Disappointed, you graciously allow her to take the spotlight. Unfortunately, this has happened many times, and the period for her spotlight may be long.

As time passes, you've lost your enthusiasm and decide, *there is no point in trying to continue what I had to say.* You look around the room, and others are also allowing Ms. Toxic to hold the floor. You think to yourself, *nobody else had interest in what I had to say anyway.* Whenever the moment to speak comes back to your court, you quickly mumble something to get it over with.

Then your best friend says something that Ms. Toxic considers offensive. You know your best friend would never say anything to offend others; this was just a misunderstanding. Ms. Toxic demeans her in front of the others. You want to speak up to defend your friend or to tell Ms. Toxic to stop, but you freeze and do not say or do anything. Nobody else speaks up on her behalf, either. You feel shame, knowing your friend has reason to believe that all are in agreement with the hurtful words spoken. You can see the tears in her eyes and imagine her pain. While you are genuinely sad for her, you're also secretly thankful that those vicious words were not pointed at you (this time). Later, you vow, *I will talk to my friend and let her know I care.*

As the time moves along into more pleasant conversations among the women, you almost allow yourself to forget those ugly moments. Suddenly Ms. Toxic interjects (or hijacks) the group with a personal and complex story. Her tale takes a while to introduce, with the drama escalating with excessive detail. You feel your mind wander, *How many times must I hear her emergency soap operas?* Then you hear her insist that she desperately needs volunteers to help.

Sheepishly and uncomfortably, people look at one another, each knowing this manipulative tactic has happened before. While the request hangs in the air each person holds their breath; no one wants to commit to help her. At the same moment you all wait for her to choose her hero of the day. You are relieved when she chooses someone else in this emergency. *Whew!* Then you immediately feel guilty that you were relieved.

After the meeting, you start to move toward your best friend, to tell her you do care and to show empathy toward her discomfort and hurt feelings. But your best friend rushes out the door and Ms. Toxic catches you, insisting that the two of you have a private conversation immediately. You give excuses why you must leave, but she is determined as she grabs your arm to stay.

There, she shares her mean-spirited thoughts about your friend, being persuasive that you fall in line with her opinion. You struggle with words to support your friend, but she shoots them down, adding to the fire with new and incriminating gossip about her. It hurts your soul to hear these damning words about your friend. Ultimately, she determines that your friend is not a good fit for the group. She demands your agreement, giving numerous instances of her kindnesses and reasons that you owe her.

Finally, seeing that your resolve has not changed, Ms. Toxic brings in emotional blackmail to threaten you: you will not belong with the group if you fail to comply, and she may feel the need to share some personally embarrassing secrets that she knows about you...

Does any part of this scenario ring true to what you have experienced? Who are the toxic persons in your life?

One thing I have learned to be true. When a toxic person comes to you with an incredible story where you are the only person who can help, beware! As their only possible hero, you must fix the problem, or use your time, money, or resources to help. In reality, they have already pre-planned who their targeted hero will be. And, they already have another plan in the works. If you decide not to help them, they will target another hero. Plan B is already set.

Think about this, as a real test: when you get away from the sight and sound of that toxic person, do you feel confused? Drained? Relieved to break free for a while? Or, are you kicking yourself with negative self-talk for letting them maneuver you into their plans?

We all have our bad days, and we may say or do something that's out of character for ourselves, but when we see that we are allowing someone to *habitually* negatively affect us, we should beware, for our own sake. Our inner peace and joy are at risk.

What do good, kind people usually do when they find themselves present within the arena of such a malignant person?

Many good, kind people think they must endure the toxicity, for many reasons. They grin and bear it, hoping for the best outcome to eventually happen. They hope and pray that this person will change. Maybe they rely on others to do the hard work toward initiating changes in the toxic environment. But unfortunately, others in that circle are probably also waiting and hoping for someone to cause a positive outcome.

I've often heard it said, "Hurting people hurt people," to encourage empathy. To a certain extent, that may be helpful for understanding the actions of some toxic people. Having empathy doesn't serve to relieve the pain and suffering experienced while in the company of a toxic person though, does it?

If it's true that the toxic person is acting from a place of hurt, does that give them a pass for bad behavior? When we're present with the toxicity and say or do nothing, aren't we implying approval for their vicious words or malicious ways? Might tough love practices be in order?

Then again, it's not always true that those who hurt others are hurting over wounds they've experienced.

Our world does have people in it who choose to be mean-spirited as opposed to kind. But even if they simply enjoy inflicting pain, we still have no standing to judge them, do we?

While we sacrifice our time, resources, money, and maybe even our reputation in our quest to be available for that toxic person, we are suffering. We are unnecessarily falling on a sword that has no good purpose or end.

This may seem to be on the opposite side of the spectrum from being totally compliant and empathetic, with neither being within the balance. I used to think that when I fell victim to an abusive or toxic person, I could and would forgive them, but sometimes I also presumed they were cruel and evil to the core of their being. This is extreme, but it might look like, "I forgive you, but you are a lost cause." While I believed I had forgiven, I judged them and wrote them off as if they were on the road to hell.

To my surprise, a person can and will treat me or someone else viciously, and yet, be kind to others, maybe to all others. That's confusing, isn't it? It remains a mystery to me, although I certainly realize everyone is not going to like everyone else, without someone having negative feelings toward another. Who knows? Maybe they have reason to feel threatened or jealous? We don't live in a perfect world; people are not perfect.

Being within the environment with a habitually mean-spirited, toxic person is similar to a domestic violence situation with an abuser. We can pray for them from a distance. We can forgive them from a distance. Our prayers and forgiveness come from the heart! They do not need to know we've prayed or forgiven. We are not supposed to remain in a continuous toxic environment.

With a toxic person, we pray, pray, pray. We go through a pattern of forgiving, getting hurt, forgiving, suffering, forgiving... on and on in an endless destructive cycle.

We know the meaning of forgiving seventy times seven as described in the Word of God. But the situation with the toxic person does not change. They may never be sorry for what they've said or done; regardless, they may never feel a reason to apologize.

That situation won't change until, or unless, we take affirmative action. What might that be? To safely get out of that toxic environment or to leave the toxic relationship. Let it go, and move on to healthier relationships with kind, positive and loving people.

I know from where I speak. I survived child abuse, which I shared with you, and I survived life-threatening domestic violence while in my forties. You can read about getting into, experiencing, and overcoming domestic violence in *My Dear Rosa Jean*. It was during my recovery that I wrote my first novel, sharing my testimony in the best way I could, using a fictional storyline.

Even after these past abuses, I allowed myself to remain in a relationship with a toxic person for years. It wasn't child abuse and it wasn't domestic violence (no physical attacks, no mortal threats, and not with an intimate partner). With a life of abuse patterns fixed in my subconscious, and personal boundaries already askew, I didn't realize what I was in. I was allowing myself to suffer abuse repeatedly by a toxic person.

Please heed to my cautionary tale and don't waste years in a toxic environment. If you are continually treated as not wanted or not good enough within a group or environment, and you see no improvement over a reasonable period of time, then you can and should gravitate instead to people who are kind and accepting. Why bring your energy and self-esteem to an expensive loss while other people can and will appreciate you?

I came to the end of my ability to endure suffering on-going heartache and sleepless nights of remembered screams at me. It's hard enough for a person without a history of post-traumatic stress disorder (PTSD) to get over another person screaming personal affronts to them, but when suffering many years of PTSD in the past, then horrible flashbacks are triggered.

As in my case, the aggressor may scream at their victim five times, but the recipient may hear it thousands of times while feeling the pain as if it is happening over and over again. I've heard such recurring screams referred to as neurological curses, but I'm not educated about that topic. Please check with a good psychologist if this is happening to you.

All the while I experienced these screams, the enemy of my past would whisper, "See, no one cares." My situation seemed to evidence (again) that I was not enough, that I was not loveable. What could I do?

I cried out to the Lord, saying, "I cast my cares! I cast my cares!" Desperately, I asked, *How* do I cast my cares?"

And, not immediately, I felt the Lord's answer in my soul, "Your season of abuse is over, and I never meant for you to remain in it."

What? I didn't realize that I had been in abuse, but that's what it was. My next thought was, but, because of who this toxic person is, don't I have to be in it? I don't have a choice, do I? After all, it's my ＿＿＿＿＿＿＿＿＿ (fill in the blank: boss, church member, in-laws, sister, etc.).

That's where the new thing I learned kicked in.

I seriously considered what the Lord had shared with me. I was *not* required to remain in that situation, no matter who it was. Considering this, I knew I should take action. We demonstrate our faith by taking affirmative action, taking a step of faith. It was hard, but courageously I let the folks within that toxic environment know that I would no longer be in it.

Thank you, Jesus!

Immediately after taking this step, my mind was at peace: no more sorrows, no more pain, anxiety, or confusion. All were replaced with inner peace. I no longer heard the screaming into the night; it had stopped.

Because of my own experience I don't believe anyone should remain in a toxic environment. I encourage you to have a serious talk with God, yourself, if you've been allowing yourself to remain in an on- going toxic environment with such abusive, toxic people like what I described. What does the Lord say to you in your situation? As you pray, meditate on His Word, and listen for His voice. He will guide you.

Some years ago, while hurting and wondering why a fella couldn't seem to love me as I loved him, I asked the Lord about it, and then went to sleep. That night I dreamed of this man sitting at the head of a table, and there was a line formed of those of us who wanted to receive his love. To my surprise, Jesus himself was ahead of me in that line. And I realized, it's not about me.

I learned that when a person doesn't care about me, and they prove themselves to be mean-spirited, it's not about me, it's about the condition of their heart. Often, their behavior is likely a sign that they have also rejected Jesus. We can forgive them, honestly praying, "Father, forgive them, for they know not what they do."

Once out of that toxic environment, I realized that I had hoped there would have been folks among the group who would have reached out to me, soothe my wounded soul, reassure me that I did belong regardless of my troubled plight. Were they afraid for themselves? Were they in agreement with the treatment? Did it seem unimportant to view as an issue?

I don't know the many possible reasons people may fail us, but to not get involved or help someone in need is the nature of man since the fall of Adam and Eve. I believe crime, decay in morals, and chaos we see around us and on television attributes to the lack of empathy in our fellow man. These people too should receive our forgiveness and prayers. It's not ideal, but those folks can also receive forgiveness and prayers without their knowledge and from a distance.

I invite you to make your own study through the scriptures

about the pros and cons relating to the character of who you let into your circle of relationships. Let me share a few:

"Don't befriend angry people or associate with hot-tempered people, or you will learn to be like them and endanger your soul."
Proverbs 22:24-25 NLT (New Living Translation)

"For wherever there is jealousy and selfish ambition, there you will find disorder and evil of every kind." James 3:16 NLT (New Living Translation)

"...bad company corrupts good character." 1 Corinthians 15:33 NLT (New Living Translation)

This next scripture should impact each of us significantly because it speaks on things that our Heavenly Father hates. We don't want any part of what He hates, do we?

"There are six things the LORD hates—no, seven things He detests: haughty eyes, a lying tongue, hands that kill the innocent, a heart that plots evil, feet that race to do wrong, a false witness who pours out lies, a person who sows discord in a family."
Proverbs 6:16-19 NLT (New Living Translation)

I encourage you to learn about the character of Jesus and then emulate him. How? By reading and studying the Word of God and praying, we come to understand Jesus. Through prayer, we're having a conversation with the Lord. We talk to him and listen for His voice, His response. We learn His expectations and obey. Because of our gratitude for all He's rescued us from, we worship and praise the Lord, as He guides us. More and more the Lord will reveal what our next steps should be. In all of this, we're developing a deeper and deeper relationship with Him.

When adversity comes, you're not alone! With God on your side, you have His strength to lean on. Cast your cares on the Lord, and

He will fight battles for you. In time, as you continue in patient faith, you will see what happens for your good, in His perfect way, and with His perfect timing. It may not look at all like what you thought it would.

You don't need to dwell on the past anymore. God has it in His hand. As I said before, you can have inner peace and joy, despite any situation or circumstance.

Scriptures encourage us to spend our time around like-minded believers, who will lift us up, not try to tear us down. We encourage each other!

"Don't team up with those who are unbelievers. How can
righteousness be a partner with wickedness?
How can light live with darkness?"
2 Corinthians 6:14 NLT (New Living Translation)

We can each deliberately strive to minimize or walk away from our relationships with habitually toxic people, and gravitate to those who are positive, loving, and kind.

We can be around those who demonstrate the character of Jesus. And we, ourselves, can strive to be more and more like Jesus.

I'd like to reiterate what the Apostle Paul said to the Philippian church because we can view it as our remedy in our dealings with the habitually mean-spirited people in our toxic environments.

"Don't worry about anything; instead, pray about everything.
Tell God what you need, and thank Him for all He has done.
Then you will experience God's peace, which exceeds anything we
can understand. His peace will guard your hearts and minds as you
live in Christ Jesus."
Philippians 4:6-7 NLT (New Living Translation) (emphasis added)

6

HOW CAN YOU HEAL FROM THE PAIN?

*I*f you were asked to identify your most painful hurts in life, what would that look like? Whatever your painful experiences may have been, I believe that something within my story will resonate with you; we can learn from past hurts together.

If I had to identify the most painful hurts in my life it would probably relate to these areas:

- Emotional pain due to loss of loved ones, whether through betrayal, death, or other reasons.
- Physical pain due to health issues or injuries, regardless of the cause.

EMOTIONAL PAIN

Have you experienced betrayal by someone who should have cared about you?

By far, the most debilitating emotional pain in my life was through the repeated betrayals of my father. I could not understand why he did not help me while I was in desperate need of his rescue from the abuses of my mother. I rationalized that he didn't love me, but I was still left with lasting confusion and sadness in my heart and mind. What about compassion for a fellow human being? If he was afraid to intervene, couldn't he have done something indirectly to prevent further abuse? Wasn't he in a position to stop it?

But then, I can recall my father telling his young children stories that he had made up; these stories were vivid, exciting, and fun to listen to. He also enjoyed taking his children to scenic parks, where we laughed and played together. He was not an evil man. Was he blind to the abuses that were in front of him? Maybe so.

During my early teens, he enjoyed when I shared science-fiction dreams with him. He had no idea how much I loved receiving his undivided attention in this. Unfortunately, it was during that same timeframe he also joined a cult.

As he and my mother fought over this new (cult) religion, they seemed to have become more deeply confused about what their own religious beliefs might be.

The last time I had told him one of my sci-fi dreams, my parents discussed at length what God was telling them in it. What did I do? I promptly decided to no longer tell such dreams, and I didn't dream sci-fi anymore. This tiny and fragile bond we had was forever severed.

As his oldest child, he brought me to his cult for training, and I began going door to door with pamphlets to promote their religion. But it was not my belief and I gradually felt more and more guilt from doing it. This cult gave lip service that Jesus is the Son of God but denied Him as part of the Trinity. What if I persuaded someone to turn from the Lord in this effort? I couldn't bear it.

I begged my father to let me stop soliciting for this cult, but any persuasion efforts were useless. We began arguing, which was not so different than the on-going arguments he had with my mother and with his family (who were of the Pentecostal Holiness faith). In the midst of that, we dealt with a major transition when it became evident my mother was mentally ill. We moved to West Virginia and she was admitted to what people now refer to as a psychiatric hospital. As the oldest child, I had to take on many more responsibilities. As for the training and soliciting, that came to an end with the transition. I found relief in knowing I would no longer speak as a false witness to others; I no longer feared that I may cause people to turn away from Jesus.

My father continued to require our family to attend cult meetings. I'd had enough; one day I decided I would not do this any longer. My father claimed he would physically force me to go. I announced, "If you get me into the car, I'll take all of my clothes off." He immediately went into a rage and beat me. Before they left for church that day, I recall my siblings looking down at me while I was lying on the floor. They silently walked out of the house and I passed out.

Among other injuries, my father had knocked my jaw out of place and choked me. I thought about this scene: he left while I was passed out; I could've been dead. I knew that if I had died, he would have "...thought the beating was for good cause; he had righteous indignation."[1]

I worked at my jaw for days (opening my mouth wide and shutting it), and it finally popped back into place. Once at school, a girlfriend saw the ring of bruising around my neck, and laughed, pointing it out to others. They all supposed the bruising was sucker bites or hickeys, and I didn't correct them. Shame is shame; what was the point in specifying how the bruising happened?

With that incident behind me, my father and I argued viciously about many things, and for a time, I think I hated him.

One evening while I prepared spaghetti for dinner, my father argued, whined, and complained because he literally expected us to eat pinto beans every day. We continued to argue at the table, and I threw a plate of spaghetti on him.

We had a violent physical fight. Afterward, I learned my siblings had been traumatized, thinking it was blood everywhere instead of spaghetti sauce. Out of guilt and shame for causing the others to worry, I cooled my jets. There were no more physical altercations although anger continued to abound. I learned to handle his negative, insulting statements by remaining verbally firm and concise in my responses; often I chose to ignore tirades of complaints and badgering. My goal was to avoid further trauma for my siblings, so I did strive to muster self-control when dealing with my father.

There was much blame and animosity in our home when my mother died. Her death was through mysterious means (which I believe was suicide); my baby brother became severely handicapped from that same incident. But at the same time we saw that, like the rest of us, my father was in great sorrow and remorse. At first, when he would come into a room, we all left, shunning him. I felt guilty in doing this, knowing he was obviously grieving. For a while, life within our home environment was strained but we pushed ourselves to be kind to him.

When I accepted Jesus as my Lord and Savior while a young wife and mother, I forgave my father for all past shortcomings. Thankfully, we were able to have a loving and kind relationship before his passing.

My first marriage failed, and I was emotionally and financially destroyed. Within months of the breakup, along came a kind and understanding older gentleman who scooped me up. He was my knight in shining armor; my gratitude toward him grew into love. We married, and he provided me the love of a husband *and* the fatherly love I had always wanted. The heartbreak over my childhood was on the mend.

Soon after we married, he pressed me relentlessly to go to college, and I acquiesced. Once I had earned my four-year degree and had worked for the Commonwealth of Virginia for two years he suddenly passed away with a massive heart attack. We knew he would probably die before me, but we never would have guessed his passing would happen in his fifties.

Have you experienced the sudden death of a loved one? It was devastating.

One evening a few months after his death, my little Pomeranian hopped onto my lap and I said to my son, "Oh, there's Rusty! Has anyone been feeding him?" My son responded, "Mom, I've been taking care of you for months, and I wondered when you'd be back. You go to work every day, but I don't know what you've been doing." Where was I during those months? I could not account for it. I went back to work just in time to save my job; I agreed to counseling. The diagnosis was chronic depression. Much later it would be discovered I also had long-term suffering from post-traumatic stress disorder (PTSD).

During the year following my husband's death, I didn't look in any of the cabinets that might have things of his in them; I didn't look into his clothes closet. I made a shrine on top of my Victrola, which included his photo and other memorabilia. So many things triggered memories that tore me to pieces all over again because of this tremendous loss. I went about like I was okay, but I was not. My heart remained broken, even while I outwardly moved on.

Grieving doesn't go away quickly, not even when we pretend it has or when we say to the world and ourselves that we're over it.

We need to allow ourselves a season to grieve so that our specific period for grieving doesn't perpetuate longer and harder than it should. What do we grieve about?

- Our loved ones are terribly missed.
- Our hopes and dreams are destroyed.
- We have regrets or unresolved hurts.

What is the designated length of time for our season of grieving? I would guess since we are each unique, the period of grieving must vary. In Ecclesiastes 3, we learn that there is a time or a season for every activity under the sun; including to be born or to die.

The Apostle Paul gave the Thessalonian church words of comfort and hope, which apply today:

"Beloved brothers and sisters, we want you to be quite certain about the truth concerning those who have passed away so that you won't be overwhelmed with grief like many others who have no hope. For if we believe that Jesus died and rose again, we also believe that God will bring with Jesus those who died while believing in Him.
This is the word of the Lord: we who are alive *in Him* and remain *on earth* when the Lord appears will by no means have an advantage over those who have already died,
for both will rise together."
1 Thessalonians 4:13-15 TPT (The Passion Translation)
(emphasis added)

When I look to the Bible for examples of people who mourned, and how they recovered, several come to mind. King David gave us two stories to demonstrate God has a good plan for our restoration and recovery. One is in 1 Samuel 30.

While David and his warriors were in battle, the Amalekites invaded where they lived, in a town named Ziklag.

"When David and his men reached Ziklag, they found it
destroyed by fire and
their wives and sons and daughters taken captive.
So David and his men wept aloud
until they had no strength left to weep."
1 Samuel 30:3-4 NIV (New International Version)

Unfortunately, many of us can relate to this. Have you ever wept until you had no strength left? At that moment, it may feel that life is over. But there was more for David to endure; the men blamed him for their loss. He felt guilty; it was his mistake to leave Ziklag unprotected. With the emotion of grief, people often attach blame or guilt toward themselves or others.

"David was greatly distressed because the men were talking of
stoning him;
each one was bitter in spirit because of his sons and daughters.
But David found strength in the LORD his God."
1 Samuel 30:6 NIV (New International Version)

King David turned to the Lord *and* he found strength because
God responded! David and his men pursued and prevailed against
their enemies, recovering all. What if David had let grief and guilt
overwhelm him, and not turned to God? The story would have had
a different ending. We too can turn to God for strength when we're
grieving, and He will respond.

Another story about King David relates to David, Bathsheba, and
her husband, Uriah, found in 2 Samuel: 11-12.

One evening, when David's men were on the battlefield, where
he should have been, David was walking on the roof. He saw
Bathsheba bathing, and he initiated an affair with her. This was the
King of Jerusalem, so I don't see a free choice on Bathsheba's part,
do you?

King David made attempts to hide that he had impregnated
Bathsheba, but because Uriah was loyal to his fellow men, he didn't
sleep with his wife. David arranged for Uriah to be killed on the
battlefield, and Bathsheba mourned over the loss of her husband.
Can you empathize with the situation and suffering she must have
endured?

The Prophet Nathan shared with King David that he had sinned
against the Lord. What were the consequences of David's
wickedness?

"Then David said to Nathan, 'I have sinned against the LORD.'
Nathan replied, 'The LORD has taken away your sin. You are not
going to die. But because by doing this you have shown utter
contempt for the LORD, the son born to you will die.'"
2 Samuel 12:13-14 NIV (New International Version)

Even though King David humbly repented, his consequences remained. David prayed, fasted, and suffered great anguish over the baby while it was sickly, but it died. Everyone was surprised that after the baby's death, David quit grieving, accepted the death as God's decision, and worshipped the Lord. Those with him were confused; they asked him how he could turn around as he did.

"He answered, 'While the child was still alive, I fasted and wept. I thought, "Who knows? The LORD may be gracious to me and let the child live." But now that he is dead, why should I go on fasting? Can I bring him back again? I will go to him,
but he will not return to me.'"
2 Samuel 12:22-23 NIV (New International Version)

One of these stories was more complex than the other, but in both circumstances, God had a plan for recovery. In each story, David turned to the Lord for strength and recovered. David's next child with Bathsheba was Solomon, who became a very wise and wealthy King of Israel, sanctified by God.

Now we know how to respond when we have a loved one who is in critical condition, and despite our prayers, they pass away. If we believe in Eternity, that eases our grief, although we miss them.

In Isaiah 61:1-3, we find that the Spirit of the Lord seeks to heal the brokenhearted, to comfort all who mourn, to give them beauty for ashes and the oil of joy for mourning. Our sorrows may last through the night, but joy comes in the morning.

We can continue in prayerful worship of the Lord, although we may not understand how the whole picture may play out in the future. We can accept that it was their time or season to go. Whether we can see it or not, God is always good and just.

These stories bring hope! We have examples of restoration for Job, Abraham, and many others. The Lord comforts those who mourn. In the Beatitudes, Jesus said:

"Blessed are those who mourn, for they will be comforted."
Matthew 5:4 NIV (New International Version)

PHYSICAL PAIN

Have you had an experience that brought you physical pain? Maybe you were in an accident, or had a physical defect to deal with? Was there a period of recovery to contend with? Are you in physical pain now? If so, I bring you hope for healing.

In 2015, I underwent therapy and various treatments, but my back pain would not let up. I remained determined not to have surgery. That is until the results of the MRI came back. I had multiple issues with discs, degenerative disease, and bundled nerves.

Before I could consider back surgery, however, I realized I must first undergo nasal surgery. I knew there would be issues with my breathing during a lengthy back surgery. I had eighty percent blockage in one nostril, and one-hundred percent blockage in the other, with various bone parts broken (I presume as a result of child abuse and domestic violence). I cannot adequately express how shockingly painful nasal surgery was. Luckily the pain was for a relatively short period, only a few days.

Once recovery from nasal surgery was completed, my doctor indicated that I might become able to smell (I lacked that sense from childhood).

One day while I was participating in a yoga class, I excitedly announced loudly that I could smell the peppermint essential oil. Of course, the others didn't understand the significance. The smell of some essential oils and the ammonia of kitty litter appear to be what I'm left with; regardless, I appreciate all that the Lord has given me, and I remain hopeful for more to come.

It took several hours to complete my back surgery with both my neurosurgeon and an ortho surgeon working together. There had been talk of harvesting bone from a cadaver to crush around the titanium; to do this reduces the possibility of my body rejecting the titanium. I was astonished to learn that the additional bone they needed was with me all along! My ruined disc and the extra disc at the end of my spine was ample supply. God had provided so they didn't need to bring in bone from a cadaver.

Have you experienced a long recovery period? If so, you know how hard it is to remain patient and upbeat during that process. I learned what it's like to remain in stages of recovery for an extended time, and about the layers of physical healing. Everything in life is a process, isn't it? Beginning with a walker, then graduating to a cane, and then wearing a four-pound full brace-vest for four months, my healing process was deemed complete within a year. Throughout this, what felt like lightning bolts could surge through my body at any moment, as my nerves healed.

I'm grateful that my pain was minimal. When I went in for my six-week checkup, my neurosurgeon asked me how much pain I was in, ready to write a prescription. I responded, "What pain?" Thank you, Jesus!

In six weeks, I was able to go back to my desk job. It was only slightly embarrassing at first to be seen by co-workers while in various stages of recovery. People did stare as I entered the hallways or elevators, and some were shocked, exclaiming, "What *happened* to you?" I was the first of many in my small division to get my desk area set for standing at my computer. The Lord was good to me.

To maintain a positive attitude through it all required patient, unfailing faith. For some time, before, during, and after this surgery, I prayed several times a day.

I knew the Lord could have miraculously healed me without surgery, but that wasn't my path; there was something for me to learn while on this journey.

There are several scriptures for healing, but this is the one the Lord gave me. I share this scripture with you knowing the healing power in it. When you pray, believing that God can heal you, your prayer is demonstrating your faith in Him.

"Heal me, O Lᴏʀᴅ, and I shall be healed;
Save me, and I shall be saved, For You *are* my praise."
Jeremiah 17:14 NKJV (New King James Version)

In the gospel of Mark 2:1-12, Jesus forgave and healed a para-lyzed man because He saw the man's faith. In faith, we too can pray to Jesus for forgiveness and healing.

Do we think Jesus can understand our suffering? He experienced more emotional pain (betrayals and rejection) and physical pain (when arrested and crucified on the cross) than we could ever imag-ine, so He does understand. Jesus allowed tremendous suffering so that He could pay for our sins; therefore, His crucifixion and resur-rection bring salvation to those who believe and accept Him. Jesus laid His life down for His sheep.

It was amazing for me to learn that once I had experienced similar emotional or physical pain, then I was better able to empathize with the suffering of others. And, I was better able to comfort them with the same type of comfort that I received from the Lord. The Apostle Paul explains this:

"All praises belong to the God and Father of our Lord Jesus Christ.
For he is the Father of tender mercy
and the God of endless comfort.
He always comes alongside us to comfort us
in every suffering so that we can come alongside those
who are in any painful trial.
We can bring them this same comfort that
God has poured out upon us."
2 Corinthians 1:3-4 TPT (The Passion Translation)

I share these stories and my testimony because I want to show you a path toward hope and healing. My prayers and empathy reach out to you if you have been suffering from emotional or physical pain, that you will find healing and peace through the Lord.

My life is proof that the power of healing from the Lord is real.

Just as 3 John was a personal letter to bring encouragement, I say this to you:

"Beloved friend, I pray that you are prospering in every way and
that you continually enjoy good health,
just as your soul is prospering."
3 John 1:2 TPT (The Passion Translation)

7

DOES SIN APPLY TO YOU?

*D*o you know there are things you're doing that are not quite right? Are you playing a game, hoping you'll get by with it? Do you want to get better?

Can you agree with me that facing hard truths may not be pleasant at the time, but later can be appreciated, and work for your own benefit? If you have the full picture before you, your chances of changing your outlook for the better are within grasp. It's all up to you.

People can be very good at fooling themselves, especially if it's to hide bad stuff. But eventually, that which we hope to hide can grow big enough to obstruct our lives, as well as that of others.

If you haven't thought about it, you may not be sure whether there are any sins, bad attitudes, behaviors, words, or actions that should concern you. But, no one on earth is perfect. Why would you need to know about the ugliness in your life? The answer is with a simple question: How can you fully initiate positive change without first taking a personal reflection to see what needs changing? And with that, how can you truly come to the Lord with penance if you see yourself with no faults?

To get straight to the worst of the worst, I hope to touch on some sins that are specifically stated in the Word of God as what the Lord hates. There are only seven deadly sins mentioned in the bible. We briefly referred to Proverbs 6:16-19 while talking about toxic people in a previous chapter. We want to know about these sins that the Lord hates, purge ourselves from them, and avoid anything that is so repugnant that the Lord detests it so greatly.

How can we hope to overcome the demons of the past, enjoy the present moment, and hope for the future if we are deeply into anything hated by God? For your benefit, let's take a look…

Personal reflection brings benefit when we know there is a remedy if we find ourselves living with what the Lord hates. To keep it brief, the seven deadly sins are:

Pride. Greed. Lust. Envy. Gluttony. Wrath. Sloth.

Pride

Do you know anyone who is prideful? Do they believe they're entitled? Do they look down on others, as if they're superior? Have you ever felt you were better than other people?

Pride seems to be operating with strength in the world today, and it can be found embedded within each of the other sins. There is a normal, balanced pride; for instance, a pride we have in our own or other people's accomplishments. That's not the same as the sinful pride described in the scripture (Proverbs 6, noted earlier).

A prideful person is full of selfishness and self-righteousness; conceited, they believe themselves as better than everyone else; they may look at others with contempt. Pride usually includes vanity, demonstrated with rudeness, and boasting. When a person conveys their belief that they are superior to others, their actions are haughty, proud, and arrogant. Often, pride goes with greed since a prideful person believes they deserve the best, even if at another's expense. Pride also ties in with envy if others have what they feel they deserve.

Do you know where pride of the heart or sinful pride started? The history of it is interesting. Drawing from Isaiah 14:12-21 in the New King James Version, Lucifer, the devil, had been a beautiful and talented angel, but he was thrown out of Heaven because of his pride. The devil was so full of pride and selfishness that he attempted to replace God as the King of the Universe. We know how the story ends when we study the book of Revelation. At Judgement Day, the devil will be cast down, as well as his followers and those who are in defiance against God.

Since pride began with the devil, it's no wonder the pride of life is one of the three main temptations our enemy uses against us (described in 1 John 2:16). A prideful heart will worship themselves, thinking they are independent of God.

The prideful will say, "Look what I have done; I am self-made and self-sufficient. Look at me!" They take all of the credit for accomplishments or successes instead of being humble, grateful, and realizing their dependence upon the Lord.

If we see that we've inadvertently failed to give God the praise for what we have, we need to quickly and humbly turn to Him with gratitude. Why?

Because a humble heart is the opposite of a prideful heart. While the Lord hates pride, He is merciful to the humble. It's in humility that we praise and thank God for what He does, giving Him the glory. With humility, we boast of our Creator, not ourselves. We know that we are but dust or vapor, and we cannot even take the next breath without our Heavenly Father. When we do good works, we do it out of gratitude, always pointing to the glory of the Lord.

Are there any consequences for people who are prideful? There are many examples in scriptures of those who faced consequences for their pride; they are cautionary tales. In 2 Chronicles 26, King Uzziah became filled with excessive pride as he grew strong, to his own destruction. In Acts 12, when Herod put on his royal robes and sat on his throne to speak to his people, they shouted that he had the voice of a god, not of a man. Immediately an angel of the Lord struck him down because he did not give God the glory.

What does Jesus say about pride? He addressed the topic in Luke 18:9-14, the parable of the Pharisee and the tax collector. The Pharisee approached God with thankfulness that he was better than others; while the tax collector humbly saw himself as a sinner, begging for mercy. Jesus said:

"'I tell you, this sinner, not the Pharisee, returned home
justified before God.
For those who exalt themselves will be humbled, and
those who humble themselves will be exalted.'"
Luke 18:14 NLT (New Living Translation)

It's scary to realize pride can be a stumbling block to keep a person from turning to God. I had a friend some years ago, whom I had assumed was a believer because he planned a Celebration of Life ceremony for his deceased family member. But he soon corrected me, saying that he had no need to turn to God. He claimed to be a good person, independent, and self-made, as his deceased loved one had been.

This outlook was troubling. Where was his hope for an eternal future? Did he believe life on earth was all there is? I was devastated; I could only cry. I continue to pray he will see the light because I know there is a remedy. He can decide to repent and accept Jesus while there is still an opportunity. Just like Hezekiah did in 2 Chronicles 32:25-26. At first, Hezekiah was proud and experienced God's wrath. But he repented of his pride, and God relented.

What the Lord said in the past holds true today. Here is a message with promise for us and for our country, from God:

"If my people, who are called by My name, will humble themselves
and pray and seek My face
and turn from their wicked ways, then I will hear from heaven, and
I will forgive their sin and will heal their land."
2 Chronicles 7:14 NIV (New International Version)
(emphasis added)

GREED

Do you know anyone who is greedy? They may have accumulated much, but do you see them still discontent and always wanting more? Will they step on you or others to get what they want?

Have you seen that in yourself?

People who are greedy are only able to see possessions as what is valuable; they seek to accumulate material wealth, money, and power for themselves. But greed is like a poison, causing the greedy person to never find satisfaction, and they will eventually self-destruct.

> "But they lie in wait for their *own* blood,
> They lurk secretly for their *own* lives.
> So *are* the ways of everyone who is greedy for gain;
> It takes away the life of its owners."
> Proverbs 1:18-19 (NKJV) New King James Version

Where is their contentment? There is none because a greedy person always wants more than they already have. They give in to temptations toward whatever irresponsible or destructive means necessary to get what they want. It's like an addiction to them. Have you witnessed it?

The phrase "the love of money is the root of all kinds of evil" is used time and time again. While the greedy may seem successful for a time, in the long run, their success ultimately runs out; regardless, it will not bring peace and satisfaction. As greed continues to grow, the objects of greed become their *gods*, eventually bringing that person to ruin. Their treasures are in stages of decay, as are all earthly treasures, and when the greedy die, they must leave their treasures behind.

LUST

Do you know anyone whose mind appears to be fixed on specific desires? Do you find their excessively lustful ways offensive? Have you ever desired something to excess?

A person who is lustful is extreme with their desires; maybe in one area or several. The three basic temptations include the pride of life (which we covered), the lust of the flesh, and the lust of the eyes (as in 1 John 2:16). We may think it only relates to sexual cravings or desires, but it can be anything we desire more than God, such as wealth. In that, lust and greed go hand in hand. Just as greed brings destruction, many a person has fallen because of the lust in their heart, whether for earthly things or desire of a sexual nature.

Is it okay to work for the attention of others through dressing, acting, and appearing in a manner designed to gain *excessive* sexual desires? You may view it as a grey area, but there is danger in it. Seduction can trigger lust, like lighting a fuse. Once lit, it's unpredictable where and how far that lust may take you. Maybe it leads to an adulterous affair, maybe deep into the emotional abyss.

Have you or other people you know found out the hard way that there are a multitude of potential consequences or unwanted results when a person is successful in triggering lust? I suggest you read Proverbs 5:3-22, which is a very interesting and detailed cautionary tale relating to seduction. When we entice lust within the heart of another or within ourselves, it can lead to calamity. A relationship based on lust lacks a sustainable foundation.

I recall a friend from many years ago who worked very hard to seduce a man she wanted into a relationship that was essentially deceptive and dependent upon his sexual lust for her. As I watched their dance unfold, I did not recognize my friend in it. Their relationship seemed to last a while until they decided to go on an extended vacation together. She could not keep up the seductive facade she had created. Once her true self was revealed, there was nothing left of the relationship. It fell apart like a house of cards. Just like greed, lust cannot ultimately bring a good or satisfying result. Surely we can choose wholesome, authentic, and kind ways to gain another person's attention, ways that can build a lasting and firm foundation.

What is the secret to contentment? This is what King David shares with us while he was in the wilderness. Satisfaction comes when our focus is on the Lord, and not on our desires or troubles:

> "I will be fully satisfied as with the richest of foods;
>   with singing lips my mouth will praise You.
>   On my bed I remember You; I think of You
>   through the watches of the night.
> Because You are my help, I sing in the shadow of Your wings.
>   I cling to You; Your right hand upholds me."
> Psalm 63:5-8 (NIV) New International Version (emphasis added)

Envy

Have you ever been envious of what another person had? Did you feel you should've been the one to have what they had? It wasn't a comfortable feeling, was it? Did you want to shout out how unfair it was?

In James 3:16-18, we find that wherever envy and strife is, there is confusion and enticement for mean-spirited or evil thoughts, words, and actions. When we envy another person, we're looking at what they have and what they've accomplished with jealousy.

We have already learned when we looked at Abraham's family that jealousy is evil and causes harm. If we allow those feelings to grow, we lust after what the other person has. We become resentful and dissatisfied with our achievements or blessings in comparison.

We see examples of envy everywhere, with the spirit of entitlement running rampant. A person with a prideful heart may set out to cause the envy of others, as they flaunt what they have. I have a simple example to share of how this plays out.

One day while shopping, I observed two women in a heated argument. Both women were physically fit and well-manicured.

They appeared to be financially well-off; both were wearing designer clothes, purses, and expensive jewelry. They appeared to have more than many women, so what were they arguing about?

One woman had something the other wanted: exquisite, expensive high-heeled shoes, the only available pair. The envious woman was angry. Even though she was late to spot these shoes and they were already in the first woman's hands, she felt she deserved them. The one holding the heels quickly became prideful and flaunted it, bringing on more strife. The bewildered clerk was expected to decide what to do. Neither of these women presented themselves well to the public in this terrible, argumentative scene. I don't know the outcome; I became disgusted at their behavior and moved on before a resolution was made.

All around us, at any given moment, we are being tempted to become envious of what another person has. And there's no sin in being tempted. Temptations will happen, just as trials and circumstances will happen. But we're responsible for how we respond to that temptation. Just like with pride, envy comes from the enemy. It is evil and destructive: there is no joy in it.

An envious person will never have enough to make them happy because envy comes from sin. Sin cannot produce lasting satisfaction for us. An envious person lacks in contentment, peace, and love. If you feel life's unfair because you don't have this or that, as you look at what others have, stop and think about it. Prayerfully, you have the power to change that attitude.

From the earlier example of wealthy women fighting over a pair of shoes, we can determine how we might handle a similar situation. When we see another person with what we'd like to have, what might be our choices to make?

What if the person in possession of the object of envy was showing off or bragging about what they had? Would that bring greater temptation? Would our decision be affected by the other person's behavior or perceived behavior?

We can decide to:

- Be sincerely happy for their blessing;
- Compare ourselves with them and wallow in self-pity because we are deserving.
- Allow envy and strife in our heart, and devise a plan to take what they have for ourselves.

We've already talked about Joseph and his brothers. They were jealous of him because he was their father's favorite. In those already tumultuous conditions, Joseph shared his two divine dreams with his brothers, which alluded to them bowing down to him (Gen. 37:5-9). Joseph might have been naïve, not realizing he was inviting envy. Maybe he was only guilty of oversharing.

Have you ever overshared? Were you so happy in the moment with the blessing you received that you failed to think about how your news may adversely affect your audience? Unfortunately, I've been guilty of this!

When we feel blessed, we're excited to share with others. In our heart, we may be thinking, "Look what God did! Our God is so good!" Sometimes it might be more appropriate to celebrate with the Lord privately. We can be mindful of how it might bring a stumbling block to those who haven't received such a blessing.

For instance, when administering to women in a shelter, would it be thoughtful or thoughtless to adorn yourself with your best clothes and jewelry? Wouldn't it be better to keep in mind the goal, which is to encourage hope, not envy; to emphasize love, not lack?

GLUTTONY

When you hear the word 'gluttony,' what do you envision? Do you presume it's all about a person being overweight?

Gluttony can come in when a person repeatedly and greedily overeats. But there are many causes for being overweight, and many do not relate to greed at all. Simply being overweight does not mean a person is gluttonous. Regardless of how another person came to be overweight, we have no place to judge, do we? These scriptures may surprise you:

"They are headed for destruction. Their god is their appetite, they brag about shameful things, and they think only about this life here on earth." Philippians 3:19 NLT (New Living Translation)

"Sodom's sins were pride, gluttony, and laziness, while the poor and needy suffered outside her door." Ezekiel 16:49 NLT (New Living Translation)

"Do you like honey? Don't eat too much, or it will make you sick!" Proverbs 25:16 NLT (New Living Translation)

The following scripture spoke to me. Yes, it is talking about our spirituality. But I believe it also speaks to the utmost reason why we should take great care of what the Lord has lent us, our bodies. I'm not just talking about what we eat or don't eat, but about everything involving our health that we may have control over. It's an important reminder for believers to make healthy decisions in every facet of life. Our health may be affected by everything we think, feel and do, as well as what goes into the body, or is ingested.

"Don't you realize that all of you together are
the house of God, and that
the Spirit of God lives among you in His house?
If anyone defiles and spoils God's home,
God will destroy him. For God's home is holy and clean,
and you are that home."
1 Corinthians 3:16-17 TLB (Living Bible) (emphasis added)

As of this writing, I am overweight, and prayerfully in pursuit of healthier living. In appreciation for the Lord allowing me to have this temporary body, I refuse to remain unhealthy in any area where I may have control. I understand moderation is often the key, but some things are a health hazard from the start.

Are there areas where you are making choices that bring on problems with your health? Is there something you can do about it? We can do nothing to improve our health without God's help. I urge you to turn to Him, and then to seek out like-minded support, with the advice of health professionals. Here is some encouragement I found from the Apostle Paul:

"I know what it means to lack, and
I know what it means to experience overwhelming abundance.
For I'm trained in the secret of overcoming all things,
whether in fullness or in hunger.
And I find that the strength of Christ's explosive power infuses me
to conquer every difficulty."
Philippians 4:12-13 TLB (Living Bible)

WRATH

Have you ever reacted to a situation to the point of extreme anger, rage, or indignation?

That would describe wrath. If allowed to flourish, wrath can bring a person to take actions as extreme as murderous intent. As humans, we are tempted to act out of anger, but how we respond to that temptation is important. We'll be talking about wrath in another chapter, "Have You Been Malicious Inside?"

SLOTH

In the workplace or at home, we've all witnessed another person who appeared to be too lazy to do their chores; they seemed to choose to remain inactive. Some slothful people may believe themselves to be entitled or 'too good' to stoop to perform the amount of labor or efforts that other people put forth. Have you ever felt like doing nothing? There is much in the Word of God regarding sloth; here is one passage as food for thought:

"Taking the easy way out is the habit of a lazy man,
and it will be his downfall.

All day long he thinks about all the things that he craves,
for he hasn't learned the secret that the generous man has learned:
extravagant giving never leads to poverty."
Proverbs 21:25-26 TPT (The Passion Translation)

We will briefly touch on this topic in the chapter, "Can You Run The Race?"

Whew! You may feel emotionally exhausted after reading this chapter. Sometimes personal reflection can be intense. This scripture seems to sum up what we've covered and why, along with promise in the end.

"Stop loving this evil world and all that it offers you,
for when you love these things you show that
you do not really love God;
for all these worldly things, these evil desires—the craze for sex,
the ambition to buy everything that appeals to you, and the pride
that comes from wealth and
importance—these are not from God.
They are from this evil world itself.
And this world is fading away, and these evil,
forbidden things will go with it,
but whoever keeps doing the will of God will live forever."
1 John 2:15-17 TLB (Living Bible)

Let's not leave this chapter without praying together, because we know there is a remedy if we find within ourselves any of these sins:

Dear Heavenly Father,
We humbly come to You to repent of our sinful living
and turn back to You so
"that our sins may be blotted out, so that times of refreshing may
come from the presence of the Lord," (Acts 3:19 NKJV (New King
James Version)

"Oh, do not remember former iniquities against us!
Let Your tender mercies come speedily to meet us,
For we have been brought very low. Help us,
O God of our salvation,
For the glory of Your name be granted us in our need.
Come restore us, for the glory of Your name; and deliver us, and
provide atonement for our sins,
For Your name sake! (Psalm 79:8-9 NKJV (New King James Version)
We pray this in the name of Jesus Christ, our Lord and Savior.
Amen.

8

HAVE YOU BEEN MALICIOUS INSIDE?

*A*s we mentioned in the previous chapter, people will feel anger from time to time and be tempted to act upon it. One situation or offense may be easy to respond to in a calm and patient manner, while another might cause extreme anger or rage. That increased anger describes wrath, one of the deadly sins. That wrath can grow to murderous intent and actions. It's amazingly scary how quickly we can go there if we're not watchful.

People who have withstood injustices in life may be more easily tempted to fall into wrath, which could grow toward intentions for revenge, to do harm, or to become malicious. It is especially important for people who have been wounded or mistreated to be able to look inside their hearts and minds. With that look inside, we may be able to deal with ugliness before it has a chance to develop further.

One day I may have a moment of anger when another person puts me down or is haughty with me, but I manage to respond well. I feel good about myself. But that same day I could be driving along and suddenly another driver cuts me off while speeding and weaving through traffic. What happens? Anger quickly grows into rage, and I yell something at them as they disappear. Well, that reaction is not so good. Fortunately, the other driver wouldn't hear me or know I had yelled at them. But for another person in this same incident, it may spur them to chase after the offender with intent to do harm. Can you relate to this?

I used the example describing "road rage" because many people seem to be triggered by the actions of another driver while on the road. Have you noticed specific situations or people that can ignite your wrath? Do you feel tempted to take vengeance on them in some way? Are you sensitive to certain name-calling? Is it because of a painful past incident? You need to know the answers to these questions and know what triggers your anger.

Here is valuable advice from the Apostle Paul:

> "Go ahead and be angry. You do well to be angry—
> but don't use your anger as fuel for revenge.
> And don't stay angry. Don't go to bed angry.
> Don't give the Devil that kind of foothold in your life."
> Ephesians 4:26-27 MSG (The Message)

That's not what many people would advise, is it? Many would encourage you to stay angry, to get even in some way, and maybe even say that you're foolish if you don't take revenge. But you probably have learned from experience that taking vengeance tends to bring trouble back to you. Only the Lord exacts perfect and just vengeance; His way and timing are perfect. Instead of trying to destroy the other person's reputation, we can consider letting the anger and bitterness go, for our own sakes.

> "Keep vigilant watch over your heart; *that's* where life starts.
> Don't talk out of both sides of your mouth; avoid careless banter,
> white lies, and gossip.
> Keep your eyes straight ahead; ignore all sideshow distractions.
> Watch your step, and the road will stretch out smooth before you.
> Look neither right nor left; leave evil in the dust."
> Proverbs 4:23-27 MSG (The Message)

What was that again? "Leave evil in the dust." I love that!

In a previous chapter, I had mentioned that I am sensitive to hearing myself or others being called or referred to as "stupid," because such name-calling was common while growing up. If in passing I hear someone being called or referred to as stupid, instantly I might be tempted to feel anger. Would it go further? Would I go into a rage? Would I have malicious thoughts? What can I do to prevent a negative reaction?

- Prayerfully being aware of this weakness.
- Knowing the enemy is a liar.
- Having confidence that I am a loved child of God.
- Depending immediately upon God's strength.

It is important to know what triggers us to go into negative directions; we need to be aware of our weaknesses. The enemy, the devil, knows all of our weaknesses, so we must educate ourselves as to what they are, too. We don't have to deal with the triggers and temptations in life alone. We can turn to the Lord, cast our cares on Him, and depend on His strength. Then, we can leave evil in the dust!

Have you ever experienced a bad day, where you were hit with one incident after another and were tempted constantly to react badly? Did all of your anger get dealt with, or did some of it linger in your mind? Maybe you pushed it down deep inside, but it was not a resolved matter.

You might have responded outwardly in good form, and onlookers would believe you to be a patient and forgiving person. But did you smolder with anger inside? Did your anger toward one specific person or group fester enough, to the point you found yourself entertaining thoughts of revenge, or to do them harm? These thoughts refer to the condition of being malicious inside.

When our thoughts are malicious, we may decide to gossip about another person, and we may feel justified in doing it. The intent is to harm their reputation, to share their secrets, or to spread lies about them. That is mean-spirited and hateful.

We may have had malicious thoughts about other people, sometimes even with evil intentions for harming them planned out. But if we didn't put it into action, we might feel our conscience is clear of any wrongdoing. But are we clear? Doesn't it all begin with the thoughts, and then our behavior or intentions? With the thoughts and intentions already in place, couldn't we quickly progress to gossip, slander, or other actions against another?

Beware! Crimes begin with free-flowing vengeful, poisonous thoughts. As Proverbs 23:7 in the New King James Version points out, "For as he thinks in his heart, so is he..." knowing that "... the mouth speaks what the heart is full of," (Luke 6:45 NIV).

Have you ever acted this out, through thought and intent, followed by a spiteful act? Ask yourself (without considering your reasons or excuses) if you've acted maliciously toward another person. Was there lasting satisfaction from it? The answer must be that if there had been any satisfaction from it, it was short-lived. How do I know? Because to decide to behave maliciously is to put evilness into action; and there is no real or lasting satisfaction to come from it.

The potential is there. You, me, all of us should take a serious look at ourselves regularly. If we allow anger to develop inside, we're only a half-step from saying or doing something mean-spirited that could harm another person, or from making a horrible mistake.

Nobody is perfect. I'm not saying this to bring condemnation, only conviction, so you can quickly turn to Jesus for redemptive mercy. As I shared already, in my past there was child abuse and domestic violence; in that arena, there was a spiritual battle going on for my soul. I know what it's like to be very angry, indignant, to mouth off terrible things in the heat of anger; to be bitter and plot to tell secrets that would do another person harm. I have been the victim of physical abuse. As a teenager, I was very angry with my father; together, we had horrible verbal and physical fights. We were both in the wrong. I was malicious inside! Thankfully I forgave my father and received God's forgiveness in that matter. As I noted before, my father and I had a nice, loving, and cordial relationship before he died. It is scary to think that if we do not control our thoughts, emotions, and actions, we can allow ourselves to be worked up to the brink of dangerous, violent, and malicious actions. When we look at the deadly sins in the New King James Version, we see wrath reaching murderous intentions:

> "These six *things* the LORD hates,
> Yes, seven *are* an abomination to Him: A proud look, A lying tongue,
> Hands that shed innocent blood,
> A heart that devises wicked plans,
> Feet that are swift in running to evil,
> A false witness *who* speaks lies,
> And one who sows discord among brethren."
> Proverbs 6:16-19 NKJV (New King James Version)

The phrase, "hands that shed innocent blood," not only speaks to wrath in action, but also to murderous intent. We know from Jesus' lecture that when a man intends to commit adultery, he has essentially already committed the deed, as far as sin in his heart (see Matthew 5:28). Not every person who screamed, "Crucify him!" took actual part in crucifying Jesus Christ, but they were still just as guilty because they were malicious and murderous in their heart.

Although it was a legal form of punishment in the land at the time Jesus was crucified, it was clearly the shedding of innocent blood. They could not get around the fact they had sinned against Him. We know it was the ultimate demonstration of evil. In today's world, if it is convenient, if we are given the rationale to do it, and if we have the permission by law to do it, is it then not sin to shed innocent blood? We each need to think about this seriously. Is an unborn baby *innocent blood*? We will find many evil things to tempt us because of convenience for ourselves. We can always find a rationale to support whatever choices we make; often the law of the land will not reflect a moral marker.

Our ultimate judge is the Lord, and He is who we need to humbly approach in repentance when we have sinned. It will not clear a person of wrongdoing, if, when facing Him, they give excuses, rationale, and quote the law of the land. These will not justify evil done to the innocent.

Can anything justify the shedding of innocent blood? In the ultimate courtroom, will the defendants be making claims to the Lord: "But it was legal! It was okay with everyone around me and with the customs of our land! It was convenient for *me*!"

While you have the opportunity, you can prayerfully ask the Lord to examine your heart, receive the gift of conviction, and let Jesus show you what is righteous or not.

When you see evil in your own heart, you can humbly repent and walk away from it. When you accept Jesus, He will cleanse you of it!

"I call heaven and earth as witnesses today against you, *that* I have set before you life and death, blessing and cursing; therefore choose life, that both you and your descendants may live..." Deuteronomy 30:19 NKJV (New King James Version)

Choose life! We have free will in every decision we make. Beware of being overly influenced when weakened in resolve. Our chances of acting out of control are magnified if we feel desperate because of the circumstances we face, or we are already worn down and tired. Our soundness of mind can also become altered if we take drugs or alcohol in excess.

How many crimes of passion have we heard about in the news? Can any be avoided? Have you ever laid hands on another? Were you sorry, or did you blame others for it happening? Did you say the lack of control was because of alcohol or drugs?

It boils down to the decisions we make when we are tempted. We control whether we allow ourselves to dwell on the transgressions of others, to plan revenge. We are in charge, even when we allow ourselves to be overtired or under the influence of a substance. As much as we can control ourselves in making sound decisions, it is good to do so; while we maintain a sound mind, we can avoid a multitude of mistakes.

"Be alert and of sober mind.
Your enemy the devil prowls around like a roaring lion looking for someone to devour."
1 Peter 5:8 NIV (New International Version)

Logically, we can learn from our past mistakes. If we have had a DUI (citation for driving under the influence) in the past, and choose to drink and drive again, we have decided to take that risk of getting another DUI, of harming others or hurting ourselves while drinking and driving. Prayerfully, we can avoid reoccurrence.

I recall making a mistake out of foolishness many years ago. I had gone to a restaurant with a date, having the intention to eat dinner with him. But while we waited for a table, he first took me to the bar and ordered me a strong drink.

The drink tasted delicious and I didn't realize what damage had been done until I attempted to get up from my stool. For many reasons I realized afterward (I was not experienced with drink, I was small in size, and I had not eaten for hours), that one drink made me feel desperately drunk. Knowing that I was indeed out of control in that state, I appealed to the bartender for help, and he fed me. While my date verbalized it was "nothing" and laughed about it, the bartender watched over me until I felt better. That foolishness could have caused me great trouble in many directions. Because I was not in control of my faculties or of a sound mind, the enemy, the devil (or my date) could have taken advantage of me in that instance to bring me shame and regret.

Statistics will reflect the likelihood that someone will repeat their specific mistakes. When we study statistics concerning our propensity to make those mistakes, we can find a helpful deterrent. For instance, in domestic violence, if a person hits their intimate partner once, chances are high it will happen again. If they hit their victim in two or more incidents, however, the statistical probability of it happening again goes up substantially. Knowing that information, a victim of one or two domestic violence incidents may find the empowerment needed to decide to leave that environment.

What am I saying? We each have the propensity at any time to turn to good or evil thoughts, words, and actions. The decision on which path we take is always there for us to make.

If we already know we have maliciousness in us, it is imperative, for our sakes, that we work on that. What can we do?

As we noted in the recipe to overcome, we first need to turn to God for help. Run to Him!

He's already aware of all our evil thoughts and past ugly words and actions. And He still loves us! We can humbly turn to Him in repentance, acknowledging Jesus paid for our sins on the cross and defeated death; and we accept Jesus as our Lord and Savior.

I had an incident as a victim to the malicious intent of another person. I complained as a dissatisfied customer and they became angry and threatened me. They said, "I will ruin you, and I have the power to do it!"

I cried. Those damning words were seared into my soul. For a while, I was fearful. And I prayed. Could they ruin me? Do they really know that much about me? I went for a few months wondering what to do.

"Teach me Your way, LORD; lead me in a straight path
because of my oppressors.
Do not turn me over to the desire of my foes, for false witnesses rise
up against me, spouting malicious accusations."
Psalm 27:11-12 NIV (New International Version) (emphasis added)

Then the Lord said into my spirit, "What do you have to be

ashamed of? Did you claim to be perfect? Haven't I forgiven you of *all* your sins? Your past is now white as snow." My resolve grew.

> "I remain confident of this:
> I will see the goodness of the LORD in the land of the living.
> Wait for the LORD; be strong and take heart
> and wait for the LORD."
> Psalm 27:13-14 NIV (New International Version)

And I knew, if God is for me, who can *stand* against me? What can man do to me? In that, I cast my cares on the Lord and walked on.

> "Praise be to the LORD, for he has heard my cry for mercy.
> The LORD is my strength and my shield; my heart trusts in him, and
> he helps me.
> My heart leaps for joy, and with my song I praise him."
> Psalm 28:6-7 NIV (New International Version)

Go to Him with your prayers and petitions and wait for His response. Whether in that small still voice, from the Word of God, or by other means, patiently, faithfully listen for His voice.

9

ARE YOU EXPERIENCING SPIRITUAL WARFARE?

*Y*es, I'm talking about spiritual warfare. It's real! If you believe in God, our Creator, then you must believe in the devil as well. That is good and evil operating in the spiritual realm all around us. Sometimes we can sense that we are stranded somewhere within that battle.

Have you experienced something in your life that you could not explain, but you know it was only by the grace of God that you were delivered from tragedy? That was the Lord's angels working on your behalf. And have you found a day that seemed to be straight from Hell, because you had unusually horrible incidents to hit you, maybe one after another? What was that? You knew it was an attack at the time. But from where? While in the midst of it, did you know what to do? Were you helpless to what may happen next?

Sometime last year while I was driving along in my little Honda Civic on Interstate 95 north in Richmond, near the Boulevard exit, rush hour traffic was flowing thick and fast. I had two buses ahead of me and a huge 18-wheeler looming closely behind me, all in the right lane. Suddenly, the first bus slammed on their brakes, and all I could do in that second is scream, "Jesus!"

The bus in front of me struggled to stop, as did I and the 18-

wheeler behind me. There was no place for any of us to go, not the other lane, and not the shoulder. I saw myself dead under the truck at that moment. But God had another plan. The bus in front of me did hit the other bus, only causing minor damages to a fender. I did stop in time, with the hood of my car closely reaching under the bus. The wheels of the 18-wheeler screeched and screeched loudly while I waited to die, and then it stopped only a hair from my bumper. If not for the Lord's hand, tragedy would have happened that day.

What was it I screamed? I think it was the shortest prayer I have ever made. The name of Jesus is powerful! He heard my cry and rescued me, just as He promises to do in the Word of God.

I've already told you about the unusual way the Lord chose to rescue me from being choked to death by my abuser; I have many more stories of how He has delivered me. And, I'm just one person. People everywhere are being supernaturally rescued all over the world. If you allow yourself to ponder on it, you will realize some things that have happened in your life, which can only be explained by His mercy.

We cannot allow ourselves to be unaware of the devil's work that is happening. We need to be aware of it. We need to be prepared for when the attack comes to us. We may cry out to the Lord for help immediately, but we may need to exercise patient faith while we wait for His rescue, just as Daniel had to wait. While Daniel's face was to the ground with a contrite heart, an angel spoke to him, in answer to his desperate and humble prayers:

"...'Daniel, you are very precious to God, so listen carefully to what I have to say to you. Stand up, for I have been sent to you.' When he said this to me, I stood up, still trembling. Then he said, 'Don't be afraid, Daniel. Since the first day you began to pray for understanding and to humble yourself before your God, your request has been heard in heaven. I have come in answer to your prayer. But for twenty-one days the spirit prince of the kingdom of Persia blocked my way.

Then Michael, one of the archangels,
came to help me...'"
Daniel 10:11-13 NLT (New Living Translation)

In this instance, Daniel, and now we received a glimpse of the spiritual battles that go on in our behalf. These battles that the Lord's angels fight for us may take time; we need to remain patient in our faith.

As I mentioned earlier, there will continue to be times when someone will behave offensively. They have free will to choose whether to respond to the suggestions of the enemy or not. When that happens, be watchful, because the enemy will whisper lies to you while you're vulnerable in hopes you will react badly or hold anger within.

How can we protect ourselves? How can we be prepared for it?

The Apostle Paul gives ample instructions to believers, to those who have accepted Jesus Christ as Lord and Savior. Paul instructs us to put on the full armor of God, so we can stand firm during spiritual battles:

"¹⁰ Now my beloved ones, I have saved these most important truths for last: Be supernaturally infused with strength through your life-union with the Lord Jesus. Stand victorious with the force of His explosive power flowing in and through you.
¹¹ Put on God's complete set of armor provided for us, so that you will be protected as you fight against the evil strategies of the accuser! ¹² Your hand-to-hand combat is not with human beings, but with the highest principalities and authorities operating in rebellion under the heavenly realms. For they are a powerful class of demon-gods and evil spirits that hold this dark world in bondage.
¹³ Because of this, you must wear all the armor that God provides so you're protected as you confront the slanderer, for you are destined for all things and will rise victorious.
¹⁴ Put on truth as a belt to strengthen you to stand in triumph. Put on holiness as the protective armor that covers your heart.

15 Stand on your feet alert, then you'll always be ready to share the blessings of peace.
16 In every battle, take faith as your wrap-around shield, for it is able to extinguish the blazing arrows coming at you from the Evil One!
17–18 Embrace the power of salvation's full deliverance, like a helmet *to protect your thoughts from lies*. And take the mighty razor-sharp Spirit-sword of the spoken Word of God.
Pray passionately in the Spirit, as you constantly intercede with every form of prayer at all times.
Pray the blessings of God upon all His believers."
Ephesians 6:10-18 TPT (The Passion Translation) (emphasis added)

Did you know the details of the armor of God before this passage? And the importance of each article of the armor used? I pray that you'll study this topic in-depth; there are many books available to help you.

To highlight, please notice:

- Verse 10 warns we are to be infused with the Lord's strength through our relationship with Jesus. With this, we can hope to stand victorious with the power of Jesus flowing through us.
- Verse 11 tells us to put on the full armor of God that He provided us for our protection as we fight the enemy.
- Verse 12 explains that our battle is not with human beings, but with demons of the spiritual realm.
- Verse 13 emphasizes again our need to wear the full armor of God provided for our protection as we confront our enemy, knowing victory is in our future.

Verses 14 through 17 describe the items of armor that a soldier would wear (using Ephesians 6:14-17 in the NIV for contrast):

"**14** Stand firm then, with the belt of truth buckled around your

waist, with the breastplate of righteousness in place, [15] and with
your feet fitted with the readiness that comes
from the gospel of peace."
"[16] In addition to all this, take up the shield of faith, with which you
can extinguish all the flaming arrows of the evil one. [17] Take the
helmet of salvation and the sword of the Spirit,
which is the word of God."

I love the shield of faith, used to extinguish the blazing arrows,
also called the fiery darts of the adversary. In faith, we can deflect
our opponent's evil intentions. In Psalms we find David's plea for
rescue, when under attack. We too can pray for our adversary's fiery
darts to fall upon themselves and that they will be exposed for their
evil plots and plans. Then they might fall to their knees to humbly
repent of their evil doings. What might these fiery darts be? Maybe
it would be gossip or other mean-spirited attacks? Or it may be
damning thoughts we hear the devil whisper to us. I hope you will
study Psalm 37, which is full of information, vital to our stand in the
spiritual battle.

How much faith do we need? As in Matthew 17:20, Jesus
explained that we only need faith to be about the size of a tiny
mustard seed, and we can move a mountain. With God, all things
are possible!

The more we stay immersed in the Word of God, the better
enabled we are for spiritual battle; the sword of the Spirit is our
weapon of protection. It is in the Word where we learn about God
and His love for us, salvation through Jesus Christ, promises and
obedience, and the key to resolving any situation or problem. I
believe what the Lord told Joshua, holds true for us today, as we
follow the Word of God:

"'Only be strong and very courageous, that you may observe to do
according to all the law which Moses My servant commanded you;
do not turn from it to the right hand or to the left, that you may
prosper wherever you go. This Book of the Law shall not depart

from your mouth, but you shall meditate in it day and night, that
you may observe to do according to all that is written in it. For then
you will make your way prosperous, and then
you will have good success.
Have I not commanded you? Be strong and of good courage; do not
be afraid, nor be dismayed, for the LORD your God *is* with you
wherever you go.'"
Joshua 1:7-9 NKJV (New King James Version)

This scripture brings encouragement and promise. As we keep
His Word, our sword and weapon, in our hearts and minds, we can
hope for our way to be prosperous and good with success. Did you
know that:

"All Scripture is inspired by God and is useful to teach us what is
true and to make us realize what is wrong in our lives. It corrects us
when we are wrong and teaches us to do what is right."
2 Timothy 3:16 NLT (New Living Translation)

Let's summarize the elements in our full armor of God. So we
can withstand the attacks of our spiritual enemy, we are to:

- Bind ourselves with truth, the Word of God.
- Wear the righteousness of Jesus that is in us through the
  Holy Spirit, including the fruit of the spirit (which equips
  us for right living).
- Be well-grounded with thanksgiving, with the peace of
  God as our anchor.
- Have faith, demonstrated by our actions to shield us from
  the fiery darts of the enemy.
- Wear our helmet of salvation through Jesus Christ, which
  is redemptive and identifies us with Jesus to protect and
  hold captive our thoughts.
- Know and utilize the Word of God, which is inspired by
  God, and *is* God speaking to us. Jesus quoted scripture as

His weapon when He was tempted by the devil in the wilderness.

Verse 18 emphasizes that we pray passionately in the Holy Spirit for all believers.

I always like to include as part of a soldier's armor, the cloak of zeal as described in Isaiah. When we go to battle, we should also be clad with divine passion or zeal for the Lord.

> "For He put on righteousness as a breastplate,
> And a helmet of salvation on His head;
> He put on the garments of vengeance for clothing,
> And was clad with zeal as a cloak."
> Isaiah 59:17 NKJV (New King James Version)

Up to this point, I have not said anything about the Pandemic that the world faces during this period of my writing to you. I worked to temporarily ignore what the news was saying about other parts of the world while my husband and I enjoyed our four-day vacation in Helen, Georgia. But then our vacation was cut short with the closing of restaurants and other businesses. We finally faced the ugly truth of this Pandemic during the week of March 15, 2020.

Before our vacation, I had been insanely stressed from the busyness that comes with an excessive schedule. I was involved in multiple workshops, outreaches, multiple podcasts, and events.

As of this writing, I have not experienced loved ones down with the Coronavirus. With the social distancing, peace came to me within the isolation, and I began to increase quality devotionals and prayer; I began to write again. I believe that it is with the challenges we face that we have the opportunity to learn valuable lessons and to mature. In light of that, I strive to impress on others the importance of turning to God for forgiveness, rescue, and salvation. Our prayers for safety and healing are essential. We can decide to be fearful or faithful. In patient faith, we can lean on the

Lord, casting our cares on Him, and through everything, to praise our Creator.

On May 5, 2020, my son suddenly passed away in his sleep; he was forty-eight years old. It had nothing to do with the Pandemic; he suffered poor health because of unhealthy choices and practices. Everyone within his extended family has been devastated.

Thankfully, he had a great testimony to share with those who grieved. He and I had many conversations about salvation. At first, he was concerned that he could never become perfect enough for Jesus to accept him. But he did realize that it was because he could never reach perfection on his own, that Jesus died on the cross for his sins, and Jesus defeated death. Jesus had waited for my son to accept Him as his Lord and Savior, not the other way around. Although we miss him terribly, it is with great confidence I share that my son accepted Jesus, and he is with Jesus now.

These scriptures were of comfort:

"The LORD is close to the brokenhearted;
He rescues those whose spirits are crushed."
Psalm 34:18 NLT (New Living Translation) (emphasis added)

Jesus said:

"'Come to Me, all you who are weary and burdened, and I will give you rest. Take my yoke upon you and learn from me, for I am gentle and humble in heart, and you will find rest for your souls.
For my yoke is easy and my burden is light.'"
Matthew 11:28-30 NIV (New International Version)
(emphasis added)

Jesus said:

"'Do not let your hearts be troubled. You believe in God;
believe also in Me.
My Father's house has many rooms; if that were not so,

would I have told you that
I am going there to prepare a place for you?
And if I go and prepare a place for you, I will come back and take
you to be with Me
that you also may be where I am.
You know the way to the place where I am going.'
Thomas said to Him,
'Lord, we don't know where You are going,
so how can we know the way?'
Jesus answered,
'I am the way and the truth and the life. No one comes to the Father
except through Me.'"
John 14:1-6 NIV (New International Version) (emphasis added)

The pastor gave an excellent sermon that honored my son's testimony and included an invitation for salvation to all attendees.

Once home, I realized an important truth that I believe is significant. In the midst of all that happened relating to this tragic event, there seemed to be very little availability for quality time with the Lord. Distractions were at every turn. The process included grieving, consoling with family, all that goes with preparing for and experiencing the funeral service, and traveling to and from West Virginia. Where was the mindfulness and time for prayerful devotionals and bible studies?

For such a time as this, it is before our trials, tribulations, or circumstances happen that we must ensure our full armor is in place. Before these events come we need to ensure we have our weapon drawn, ready for what we may face. The enemy, the devil is well aware of the hard life-happenings that come, such as the loss of a loved one. It is during those hard periods that the enemy counts on our defenses to be weakened.

What is our weapon? The Word of God! The Word of God is alive and must be well-studied and well-integrated in us. Did Jesus have His bible with Him while in the wilderness, facing the devil?

No, but He did have His weapon drawn; He quoted scriptures, as needed.

Have you accepted Jesus, but don't understand everything that it means for you?

This world has much evilness happening all around us, but God doesn't want any of us to fall. In addition to the full armor of God, those of us who have accepted Jesus Christ as Lord and Savior have received the Holy Spirit. In Him, we have renewed minds! We've gone through--and continue to go through a transformation; we are ever-changing as we mature. We are born again; we have been saved by the precious blood of Jesus. Our bodies have become temples of the Holy Spirit, and He dwells in us. We're never alone.

What does the Holy Spirit do? He is guiding and directing our decisions every step of the way, interceding in our prayers when we do not know how to pray, and comforting us as we face life happenings. When we feel a twinge of guilt or that gut feeling as we're about to say or do something, that's the Holy Spirit warning us.

Because we have free will, we can be open to developing the attributes and character traits of Jesus. The Holy Spirit provides us with the fruit of the Spirit, enabling us to become more and more like Jesus. What is the fruit of the Spirit that's available to us?

"But the Holy Spirit produces this kind of fruit in our lives:
love, joy, peace, patience, kindness, goodness, faithfulness,
gentleness, and self-control.
There is no law against these things!"
Galatians 5:22-23 NLT (New Living Translation)

How do we develop this fruit of the Spirit that's given to us? As we continue to pray, read, and study the Word of God, obey, and worship Him, then our fruit is developed more and more. We are well equipped to grow in this fruit and do good works, serving the Lord when we serve those in need, always pointing toward His Glory.

Are we supposed to only utilize what the Lord gives us for

ourselves and our families? Or, are we designed to help others as well? As we become more like Jesus, it will be more in our character to desire to serve Him in some capacity. Here is the greatest commandment that was originally shared in the Old Testament (Deuteronomy 6:5), and then by Jesus with a second commandment added:

> "Jesus replied, "'You must love the Lord your God
> with all your heart,
> all your soul, and all your mind.'
> This is the first and greatest commandment.
> A second is equally important: 'Love your neighbor as yourself.'
> The entire law and all the demands of the prophets are based on
> these two commandments."
> Matthew 22:37-40 NLT (New Living Translation)

When we love our neighbors as ourselves, we are willing to help those in need, like in the Parable of the Good Samaritan. In further scriptures, we learn that the term "those in need" is inclusive of helping those who are poor, old, widowed, and in prison.

Jesus also gave the great commission:

> "...'Therefore, go and make disciples of all the nations,
> baptizing them in the name of the Father and the Son and
> the Holy Spirit.
> Teach these new disciples to obey all the commands
> I have given you.
> And be sure of this: I am with you always,
> even to the end of the age.'"
> Matthew 28:19-20 NLT (New Living Translation)

Yes, Jesus instructs us to utilize what we have been gifted with to help or serve others. We serve by helping those in need and by sharing the gospel, the good news. Jesus himself came to earth to serve the Heavenly Father, and to serve people. We can look at what

He did as our example for life. In every instance, we can consider, what would Jesus do?

What else are we provided with while spiritual warfare happens all around us, and as we strive to help others in need and to share the salvation message?

The Holy Spirit also empowers every follower of Jesus Christ with specific Spiritual Gifts so we can accomplish good for the Lord, and they are tied in with the great commission. When we read Romans 12, Ephesians 4, and 1 Corinthians 12, we find several of the Spiritual Gifts listed.

Some Spiritual Gifts are:

exhortation, giving, mercy, prophesy, service, teaching, discernment, faith, healings, knowledge, miracles, tongues, interpretation of tongues, wisdom, administration, apostles, evangelism, and pastors.

Do you know what your specific spiritual gifts might be? Maybe some gifts are only for a season of time? You can ask the Lord about it and wait for His answer. Meanwhile, this would be a great topic to explore and study.

The Lord has surely provided for each of us in a multitude of ways. We have the Holy Spirit always with us; He equips us with the fruit of the Spirit and specific Spiritual Gifts. And, we each have the opportunity to put on the full armor of God so we can stand when the enemy attacks. With the Lord on our side, we are well able to handle whatever the enemy brings.

10

WERE YOU OPPRESSED?

*W*hen I speak of being oppressed, my thoughts are about the effects of abuse a victim in a domestic violence situation has endured. This includes an on-going and over-whelming burden, all as the result of the cruel power over them, exercised by their intimate partner. Because of the perceived abuser's power, the victim may have felt their relationship as a master and slave situation.

Have you had to endure such oppression? Have you broken free from the effects of it?

You may be surprised at the wide gambit of abuses that may happen within a domestic violence arena. Some wounds may take a very long time in healing psychologically, emotionally, and physi-cally. You may recall, I've already alluded to a period of my life (while in my forties) when I was in a serious, life-threatening domestic violence situation. I faced many debilitating abuses that I will not be describing here, except for the story about my unwanted tattoo.

Why am I talking about this specific form of abuse? Because through this story, you can see the hopelessness and permanency in scarring; and yet, the Lord had another plan for me. I hope that whatever similar situation you may have faced, you can resonate and find hope for your positive change in outlook.

You may be surprised to learn that if in that domestic violence arena the abuser compels their victim (against their will, by unreasonable pressure or perceived force) to get an unwanted tattoo, it would be considered a form of domestic violence. The unwanted tattoo is essentially as a permanent mark, wound, or scar to the victim's body, representing the scarring to their soul.

Always plotting and planning new and different ways to oppress me or others, one day my abuser decided I would get a tattoo.

Even though I was living a sinful life with this man, I came from a religious background and remembered the scripture about the body being the temple of God. In light of that scripture, I presumed (incorrectly) the reference related to marking my body (such as with a tattoo), as sin.

While having that belief, I was not willing to get a tattoo. But my resistance with fear of God's condemnation only fueled his demands for this to be done. Abusers love to push their victims to go beyond their boundaries, harming their sense of right living, and jeopardizing their moral compass. The abuser's pleasure is in successfully forcing their will upon their victim, to cause their victim to act in breach of their moral boundaries, especially if the victim abhors that action.

He continued day and night with the arguments, threats, and beatings until he broke me down. Like the cat playing with his mouse, he knew it was only a matter of time for me to comply. I was living in fear constantly during those times, and I finally acquiesced to the tattoo plan. I felt I had merely borrowed a moment from harsh punishment and pain or potential death. Added to my sorrow and condemnation of it was the sense of cowardice.

Then he announced that my tattoo would be a Geisha, covering most of my back. In this, the meaning was clear: I was a slave, like the Japanese slave, *his* slave. He proclaimed that even if anything happened so I could escape him, nobody else would ever want me. My body would be permanently marked as his slave. I believed that nobody else would want me. I was devastated to even be doing this, still believing it a sin, but it reached greater levels of pain with the meaning of it, and that it would cover such a large area. The thoughts of this impending permanent destruction to my body brought me excruciating pain.

The process of completing this tattoo took several visits that lasted for hours, having periods between visits for the open wounds to heal. He was with me as if for support. With him by my side, I had to sign a document that this process was not under duress or impairment. As I laid helpless on the table during the process of many needles piercing my skin repeatedly, I remained in deep mental, spiritual, emotional, and physical torture, unable to utter a word of objection.

Finally, the deed was done. I was overwhelmed with shame, guilt, and regret.

As you know from previous chapters, the Lord did help me escape this abuser. I asked for and received forgiveness of all my sins; I knew, if there had been any sin in my getting this tattoo, that sin was included. All was washed away by the Blood of Jesus.

The enemy tried to convince me that my life was permanently destroyed and void of any happiness in the future. But the Lord kept me under His wing and brought me out from self-condemnation and the pain of other people's judgment. How did the Lord turn it around? How could He?

Years after my abuser was gone from me, I still had the tattoo to deal with during my long recovery process. I relooked at scriptures and I realized that God cares about what is going on inside the body: the heart, soul, and mind. It appeared then, this scripture about my body being the temple of God addressed infidelity, matters of the heart, soul, and mind, and not about what adornment there may be on the outside of the body. That brought solace for me.

But all that happened more than a few decades ago, at a time when tattoos were not popular, especially on a woman, covering much of her back, and with the tattoo being a Geisha. Even without damning beliefs, I hid my back in shame. When I did attempt to do normal activities, like to go swimming or to exercise, I was harshly judged. To some, the Geisha implied prostitution. Regardless, the tattoo itself at that time implied loose and wild living.

The most painful moments came unexpectedly. While in an exercise class at the YMCA, I had enjoyed getting to know a very smart and kind older woman. But later, when she saw me wearing a towel to the showers, she suddenly glared right through me. For the moment, I had forgotten my tattoo on my back, but while showering, I realized she had seen it. Although I saw her several times afterward, she never spoke to me again.

Another time, I had been with a girlfriend walking toward the beach area at a park in my bathing suit when a very nice-looking man smiled as he passed me. But when he saw my back, he shouted angry obscenities, ending with, "I can't believe *that!*" (pointing at me). Again, I had forgotten about the tattoo.

I had tried to get insurance coverage for grafting over the tattoo, but could not; regardless, the result of the surgery would appear like severe burn scarring. I found there may be reconstruction surgery available in California, where situations like mine were recognized as domestic violence abuse, but I had no financial means of pursuing that option. I researched laser surgery but there were no guarantees, especially when the tattoo includes reds and oranges. All processes were expensive with long-term healing. It did not seem to line up with my hopes of recovery if I had to focus on the negatives of these processes long-term.

What does the Serenity Prayer say? I resolved to find a way to accept what I could not change. The tattoo, wound, or scar will remain; but how will I face the future? Will I have a pitiful tale or a testimony? The choice, whether to see darkness or the light in any outcome, is always up to each of us. Will I let the judgment of myself or others define me? Or will I turn to God for my strength?

What will you decide to do when you face such a quandary?

While in recovery I had time to reflect; I realized I had judged people harshly because of the tattoos they wore. It is shameful to realize I had allowed such a petty thing to bring me to judge another person, a stranger; that is before mine happened. I remembered that I had a major change of heart during my process. I met many nice people waiting and mingling in the parlor as customers and as I became acquainted with the artists who were performing the service. Each person was kind, sincere, and humble. None were wild or mean-spirited, as I had originally anticipated.

What type of people did I see getting tattoos? It was customers who came to adorn themselves with artwork, just as many people adorn themselves with piercings, jewelry, clothing, or hair color. Using this method, colorful inks to selected areas of their bodies, was their personal and unique expression for themselves, and some-times to the world. I could almost hear the Lord saying, "Judge not, lest ye be judged!"

I had been judged, just as I had judged. I deserved it -- and I learned a valuable lesson from it.

And then, a strange thing happened. For a brief two-year period in my life, I had begun dating a man who was a member of a Honda motorcycle group, which was composed of men and women of many ages, and their children. It was a pleasant family-oriented motorcycle group (another judgment or bias had been destroyed). Suddenly, not only were my 'tats,' okay, but they were believed to be beautiful and something to envy. With this change in attitude in the environment around me, I was no longer ashamed of my body and my self-esteem became more balanced.

I studied the definition of Geisha, and I walked away with a more positive stance. I decided to view a Geisha as essentially a Japanese hostess, trained to entertain with conversation, dance, and song. I determined that I can identify with this after all.

As we all know, 'tats' have become quite popular in recent years, so my faded Geisha is as nothing to other people now. I rarely even remember that I have it. I marvel, what an interesting way the Lord worked it out for me to gain a sense of self-worth, belonging, and healing through this issue. He truly is all-knowing and good.

Most importantly, my spiritual growth was happening. Especially through faithfully studying the Word of God, personal prayer, and fellowship with other believers, I had learned who I am in Christ. I am a loved child of God, His work of art. In various versions of the passage in Ephesians 2:10, a believer is referred to as God's workmanship, masterpiece, handiwork, and (beautiful) poetry. God loves me, all of me ('tats' and all), and I am completely His work of art, or His beautiful poetry – from the bottom of my toes to the top of my head. Thank you, Jesus!

Always remember, the enemy is a liar. When he says you are not enough or unworthy and tries to pile on you shame and condemnation, do not accept it. When our God is with us, and when our God is for us, who can stand against us?

My abuser had partnered with the devil and used my spiritual beliefs (however misled) against me so I would believe myself condemned by God. He thought I would never survive it. But I knew about the power in the Blood of Jesus!

"We are hard pressed on every side, but not crushed; perplexed,
but not in despair;
persecuted, but not abandoned; struck down, but not destroyed."
2 Corinthians 4:8-9 NIV (New International Version)

I was down, but not destroyed. My enemy had miscalculated. He did not know that in my despair that I would turn to Jesus for mercy and rescue. He did not realize that the Lord had waited for me to turn to Him for help and that He would restore me and lovingly protect me under His wing. The enemy did not realize how truly awesome and just God is!

Have you ever found yourself moving along your journey, thinking life was good and you were at peace, and then suddenly, your whole world was pulled out from under you? You may have been devastated, broken, in horrible emotional pain and in a dark place, feeling alone and hopeless...

But then, maybe not right away, you realized that you were not destroyed. You were not alone. While approaching the depth of the dark pit, you felt a spark of hope. The Lord had mercy on you and helped you. You survived to see another day. The Lord had scooped you out of your troubles, and that should not be taken lightly or ever forgotten.

What was it that brought you to the brink of destruction? It could have been bad news about a loved one. It could have been the rejection of those you love and admire. It could have been evil, calculated oppression.

The good thing to know is that Jesus knows exactly how it feels to be hurt, rejected, abused, betrayed, lied to and about, and shamed. He experienced it all – and so much more, for us! He suffered for hours on the cross, for our sakes, to pay for our sins when He had none. Jesus defeated death and He's right there with us when we believe and accept Him as our Lord and Savior. He gives us hope for a future, an eternity with Him. As in Isaiah 54:17, for those who believe and serve Him, no weapon formed against us will prosper. We are not alone.

During a recent devotion, the Lord brought a revelation to my heart. It was not just for my benefit, but to be shared with you.

The enemy used my need for a sense of belonging as a weakness. Through every adult experience where I was rejected by an individual or several people (whether a church, business, loved ones, friends, or potential friends) God allowed it to happen. He allowed it to happen so that I could:

- Learn obedience and reliance upon the Lord.
- Learn empathy toward others who may suffer from the same need to belong.
- Use the instance as an opportunity to mature along my walk.

The extent of my emotional pain, which was found in enormous betrayals, rejections, and on-going strife, was because of my stubbornness and fears of not belonging. I had to recognize and accept the door had been shut to that relationship. Admittedly, I only conceded once the situation had proved to be unbearable. In all of it, I did not sufficiently put on the full armor of God (as in Ephesians 6). Especially, I had failed to have my weapon drawn—the Sword of the Spirit, which is the Word of God.

While I listened to the Lord, I envisioned myself walking upward along a familiar dirt pathway. Nearly fifty years ago, that was a driveway leading to our isolated home on a mountainside in rural West Virginia. I saw myself wading a creek as a teenager at my Grandfather's farm with the Lord's radiance all around me while Jesus and I enjoyed the conversation.

I realized these were precious memories of quality time I had spent with Him. After this experience, I rejoiced knowing to whom I belong; I belong to Jesus Christ, my Lord. He is all I need.

If you can resonate with what the Lord brought to my heart, please join me in prayer:

Dear Heavenly Father, my Creator,
I rejoice always in You. You are my strength in times of weakness.
Your ways are always good; Your love has no end; and
I belong to You.
Dear Lord, please slam shut the doors that
I am not supposed to walk through.
Please guide me with a heavy hand. I ask for wisdom and
discernment as I study Your Word.
When I waiver, please help me to quickly fall into agreement with
Your plans so I may enjoy abundant peace
that only comes from You.
Always, I thank You for Your grace through Jesus Christ.
In Jesus' name I pray,
Amen

Whatever the situation, we can praise the Lord, pray to Him, and sincerely express our gratitude for what we now have, and for what hard times we've been brought out of. Even if the situation or circumstance has not changed, we are able (because we have free choice) to change our focus from our problems to a focus on the Lord. We can cast our cares (our worries, stress, or anxieties) on Him, knowing that He cares for us. What results from this? We receive His peace.

"'I leave the gift of peace with you—My peace.
Not the kind of fragile peace given by the world,
but My perfect peace. Don't yield to fear
or be troubled in your hearts—
instead, be courageous!'"
John 14:27 TPT (The Passion Translation) (emphasis added)

11

WILL YOU REAP WHAT YOU SOW?

*H*ad you heard about sowing and reaping before reading this title? What did it mean to you? Sowing and reaping have everything to do with the choices we make, and our intentions behind those decisions.

If you come from a life of farming, then the concept is likely easier for you to imagine. During Jesus' time, many of the people had their own farm or garden to manage. Jesus probably used parables about sowing (planting good seeds) and reaping (a harvest) so that listeners could relate the planting or sowing to decisions we make, and reaping to the results of those decisions. Please study these parables found in the gospels of Matthew 13:1-23, Mark 4:1-20, and Luke 8:4-15.

When we talk about sowing and reaping, we're addressing the choices we each make, and the corresponding results, based upon those earlier decisions. We must address the spiritual or natural law of "free will" God chose not to make us as robots who are only able to take commands; we can think and make decisions on our own. He wants us to willingly come to Him. We decide whether we sow good seed, listening to the Lord's guidance, or we will sow bad seed in reaction to temptations. The corresponding reaping will either be a great harvest or be a moment to face the consequences.

When it came time for Jesus to suffer until death on the cross, despite being the Son of God and having the power to stop it, He decided to follow the will of our Heavenly Father. Jesus knew His crucifixion and resurrection were necessary to pay for our sins. Jesus said;

"Father, if you are willing, take this cup of agony away from me. But no matter what, Your will must be mine."
Luke 22:42 TPT (The Passion Translation) (emphasis added)

As a broad introduction to this topic of sowing and reaping, I'd like to take a short trip down memory lane. Please travel with me:

During my early years, I recall going to vacation bible school during the summers at the local Baptist church. The emphasis there seemed to be on singing songs about Jesus, making crafts, and playing games. I especially loved the game, "Draw Swords," where the winner was the one who found specific scriptures first in their Bible. To this day I can quickly look up scriptures as a result of playing "Draw Swords." A few times, my sister and I went to a Pentecostal Holiness Church while visiting our cousin in West Virginia. There, when the pastor said, "Let us pray," we learned that it was a cue for the folks to open up to all kinds of worship: yelling, bobbing heads, speaking in tongues, laughing, crying, stomping, and clapping hands. My sister and I would sit in the pew back to back, earnestly praying for our safety. We were simply not accustomed to or lacked experience with other ways of worship. We later learned that speaking in tongues and making the other physical gestures we saw was a regular part of worship within the Pentecostal Church.

Early into my adult years in rural West Virginia, I also had some exposure to backcountry "hellfire and brimstone" churches whenever my sister and I went. Always, the pastor's screaming would bring fear to the congregation, especially to folks like me, who didn't fully understand concepts and terminology in the scriptures.

In all of this, my background told me that I'd better be good and obey the Lord's commandments; if not, God may throw me into hell, where I'd suffer forever.

That line of thought is precarious. We are not perfect, so we can't always be one hundred percent good and obedient. It's impossible! I had reasoned to myself, then, if I happened to be good and God was happy with me at the moment I died, I'd go to heaven. That's great, isn't it?

But what if I was not good or God was otherwise mad at me at the point of my demise? Would I go to that horrible place called hell, for eternal torment? That line of thinking seemed to fit in with my life of child abuse; I never knew when I would be punished or treated kindly. I did not realize that God is radically different in character than my parents. God loves me unconditionally, consistently; His ways are always good and just.

I can never be good enough to make it to heaven on my own, but when I asked the Lord to forgive my sins and I accepted Jesus, all of my sins were erased. Jesus, the only begotten Son of God, paid the price for my sins, and that brought me into the fold as a believer.

Jesus died and rose again; He defeated death, making it a reality for His blood to cover my sins. How long can I count on His payment for my sins to be good? As a believer, I belong to Jesus for all of my life! Nothing can take me away from the love of God; Jesus paid the price for my sins once, and for all.

Otherwise, even if I belong to Jesus and I make a mistake, that mistake could result in me being barred from heaven. If that were the case, then Jesus would have come to earth, suffered, and died, even defeating death, for nothing. The shedding of His innocent blood would be meaningless, and I'd have to revert back to the happenchance view with my destination determined by being good or bad in the moment of my last breath. But, as we already noted, I can never be good enough to make it to eternal life without becoming a believer, without belonging to Jesus, without Jesus covering my sins with His Blood.

We have all seen the unexplained phenomenon of good things

happening to bad people, and of bad things happening to good people. Only God knows the secret truths there and He's not compelled to share everything with us. Faith tells us there is an ultimate good, His will, being accomplished.

I've learned through experience that when trials, circumstances, or adversarial conflicts come to me, I'd better be quick to listen and slow to speak or respond. And in making that choice, I'm sowing what will be reaped later. A quick, emotional reaction will not fare well for me in the long run.

Have you learned this, too?

When hardship of any kind comes, we can strive to view it as an opportunity to demonstrate faith, to see in it what there is to learn so we can be empathetic in that area to help others in that same place. In other words, we can choose to determine, "How can I use this instance to sow seeds?"

When the trials come, we need to continue rejoicing, praying, being thankful, and worshiping the Lord. He knows the whole picture while we only see the moment. He works it out for our good.

I may be showing my age when I recall a phrase that was popular while I was a young wife and mother, "God will get you for that." It was often said on the 1970's television show, "Maude." Who knows? That phrase may have originated from pastors, meant as a stiff warning that a person had done something deserving of the Lord's punishment, or was involved in a serious matter from which they should repent.

I heard "God will get you for that" often coming from the Maude character with the voice of a strong and opinionated woman. But as that phrase was used more and more, the luster seemed to wear off, and people took the phrase lightly. They left it as a simple, burning retort from one person to another, letting the other party know they were not happy with their statement, behavior, or actions.

Have you seen the truth (principle) of a person reaping what they had sown? Have you seen a person regret having spread gossip about another person? Have you experienced the pain in a broken relationship because of the lies your friend told? How about witnessing the penalty imposed on someone caught in a theft? Was it a friend or loved one who brought to themselves consequences? Has it happened to you?

We can look around and know from examples before us that if we sow bad or evil seeds through our mean-spirited ways and remain in it (not turning away or changing from it), we know we will face consequences. Simply by choosing that evil, we place ourselves within that evil realm, essentially telling the Lord to stay out of it.

There's much in the Bible, beginning with Adam and Eve, regarding the choices we make; whether good or evil, we can expect to reap from what we've sown. If we sow what is good, such as good plans or works, and kindnesses, we can hope for a harvest, answered prayers, blessings, and rewards. But if we sow into our lives what is bad, unsavory, and evil, maybe mixed with greed, revenge, anger, wrongdoings, and ugliness, then we can anticipate terrible results. Those consequences may not happen immediately, or they may not be lasting; unfortunately, some consequences are permanent or deadly.

I have shared some of my reaped consequences, especially the events that followed my turning my back on the Lord and choosing a sinful life. For a time, I was allowed to wallow in the evil world I had chosen, and each moment in it was horrible.

My consequences were hard in their own way, although not permanent. I have learned valuable lessons through it all. I had sown evil into my life through a series of bad choices. Through His merciful forgiveness, I walked out from it all with gratitude for His love and mercy in a Father's correction and guidance. Thank you, Lord!

"Now no chastening seems to be joyful for the present, but painful; nevertheless, afterward it yields the peaceable fruit of righteousness to those who have been trained by it."
Hebrews 12:11 NKJV (New King James Version)

How different my story would have been had I not turned to the Lord when I did. How different it could have been for many who have had the opportunity to turn, but they refused. Or maybe they only meant to put off making that decision. But there's danger in procrastinating making a good decision because we don't know or control what may happen next. Here are some "what if" examples we can relate to:

- A man has already received charges for DUI (driving under the influence), but he decides to drive drunk this one last time. But with that incident, he is caught by law enforcement after causing a wreck, maybe with a fatality. What are his consequences?
- A woman begins to feel guilty about an affair, but she puts off deciding whether to break it off until after this one last meeting. But during that meeting, she is caught. What are the penalties for her actions? Maybe she suffers the heartbreak of a divorce with no opportunity to reconcile, precious lost time with her children, or loss of income and possessions. Maybe the incident ignited violence.

In every decision made to sow bad seeds, we see danger in not making a timely correction. In every situation in life, I believe there is always the gift of conviction, the opportunity for a decision to address the issue and make a positive change, but sometimes it goes ignored.

"Make no mistake about it, God will never be mocked!
For what you plant will always be the very thing you harvest. The harvest you reap reveals the seed that was planted. If you plant the corrupt seeds of self - life into this natural realm,
you can expect to experience a harvest of corruption.
If you plant the good seeds of Spirit-life
you will reap the beautiful fruits that grow
from the everlasting life of the Spirit.

And don't allow yourselves to be weary
or disheartened in planting good seeds,
for the season of reaping the wonderful harvest
you've planted is coming!
Take advantage of every opportunity to be a blessing to others,
especially to our brothers and sisters in the family of faith!"
Galatians 6:7-10 TPT (The Passion Translation)

What we sow is important! We will reap or receive as according to what seeds we've planted into it. When we plant good seeds by acts such as treating people with respect or giving good gifts of time, money, or labor for those in need, we can hope to reap a harvest of rewards and answered prayers. Here are a few scriptures from Proverbs that speak on wise sowing toward those in need:

"Every time you give to the poor you make a loan to the Lord.
Don't worry—you'll be repaid in full for all the good you've done."
Proverbs 19:17 TPT (The Passion Translation)
"When you are generous to the poor, you are enriched with
blessings in return."
Proverbs 22:9 TPT (The Passion Translation)

In Ecclesiastes 3, we are reminded that there is a time to sow, and a time to reap. In between the two times, we have the opportunity to demonstrate patient faith while we wait.

Our sowing of good seeds may last a very long time; it might be easy to quit believing answered prayer will happen. Especially if prayers have been going up for years with no sign of the harvest coming. In other translations of the verse we just read, Galatians 6:9, we're encouraged that we will reap a harvest "if we do not lose heart" (NKJV) or "if we do not give up" (NIV).

There are many stories of artists and authors, for example, who passed away before their works reached fruition. Vincent Van Gogh sold one painting while alive, but twenty years after his death, his artwork received recognition. I have on-going petitions to the Lord for all of my loved ones to be saved, but especially, I pray for all the young ones (grandchildren, nieces and nephews, and extended families) to have a great calling in the Lord. I believe it will happen, but I may not live to see the completed harvest happen while I'm on earth.

Maybe you are investing in a business that doesn't seem to be a success; not, at least, by the world's standards or measure for money, prosperity, or wealth. But maybe that business is already a great success in God's Kingdom because it is geared to help others in some way. Maybe you are reaping a harvest right now, and haven't fully realized it because you are simply not evaluating the progress while using the right measure?

My faith-based podcast, "Turn to God with Carin" has been ongoing for over three and a half years to date. Sometimes there's the temptation to look at the number of listeners in comparison with other podcasts, and I could become discouraged as their numbers are much higher. But we already know that comparing won't bring positive results. If only one person responds to the good news of Jesus, my efforts are worth it.

If only one person joins the Kingdom of God because we allowed ourselves to be used as His vessel, then our efforts are worth it. And we know, someone spoke to or prayed for Billy Graham; someone spoke to or prayed for Martin Luther King. Seeds were sown!

What if you sow seeds and reach one specific person, and that one person is instrumental as a great vessel to open doors for many people to come to God's Kingdom? How awesome would that be?

We do not know the timeframe between our sowing and the resulting reaping, but we can trust that God will answer our prayers and someone will benefit from the planted good seeds. We need to be steadfast with our patient faith that the harvest will come. If we really believe that as we give, we will receive "pressed down and in good measure," then how much effort are we putting into it?

Did you volunteer to help someone? Maybe at that moment you were excited and sincere, but as time elapsed, you became busy, distracted, and feelings changed to boredom, discouragement, or disinterest? What happened? Did you lose your zeal or enthusiasm in that endeavor? Did you quit? What then, can you hope to reap? What will that harvest look like if you have given up?

What if you don't actually give up; but instead, your interest in it wanes significantly? What would that harvest look like?

We have an issue to consider as we sow good seeds. What is our motivation, and does that motivation matter?

> "Here's my point. A stingy sower will reap a meager harvest,
> but the one who sows from a generous spirit will reap
> an abundant harvest.
> Let giving flow from your heart, not from a sense of religious duty.
> Let it spring up freely from the joy of giving—
> all because God loves hilarious generosity!"
> 2 Corinthians 9:6-7 TPT (The Passion Translation)

The reasons behind sowing need to be addressed authentically. We can ask ourselves, "Why am I doing this? Is it coming from the heart with a sincere desire to help others, to make life easier or better for them? Or, am I doing this good deed to be praised by others for my generosity and goodness?" Upon our self-examination, we may find that our reasons for doing good are a mixture of wanting to glorify God *and* to impress others.

We can easily fall into a trap, can't we? Even if we start out with noble intentions, the world can quickly put a spin on what we're sowing. We can become distracted when we hear flattering words about our good deeds. We may begin with no thoughts of a reward, but if there would be a reward, we would hope for eternal rewards from heaven. But, might we end up with merely momentary earthly rewards? If the sower is not careful, it can become difficult to remain focused upon the purpose and to know where the line is drawn (as I can relate to), especially when:

- We share our efforts with the initial intent to encourage others to join in helping those in need.
- We inadvertently receive verbal or material rewards from on-lookers for our good efforts.

We need to always remain mindful of the purpose of our sowing to ensure intentions remain good and pure. That would entail consistent conversations with the Lord, and having an openness to receive the truth about ourselves. How easily we can be swayed by public recognition if we are not careful! The choice is ours. If we lovingly give generously of our time, money, or resources to help others, we know where our rewards come from. When we sow good seeds, a harvest comes, but will that harvest include a reward from heaven with permanence (forever), or a temporary reward on earth (various accolades)?

"'Watch out! Don't do your good deeds publicly,
to be admired by others,
for you will lose the reward from your Father in heaven.'"
Matthew 6:1 NLT (New Living Translation)

In this chapter, we have looked at the ultimate sown decision found in our choice to accept Jesus with heavenly reaping, the consequences of reacting to worldly temptations, and the harvest in our response to do good and to help others. Here's another area to consider: If you decide to sow thankfulness into your life, to choose to be filled with gratitude toward the Creator of the Universe, what will you reap, even while you sow?

When we rejoice in everything, we're being obedient to the Lord, acknowledging dependence upon Him, and appreciating all that He has done and is doing for us. In that instance, there is no room for discontent, complaints, and temptations; in that instance, we enjoy peace and blessings.

"You are my strength and my shield from every danger.

When I fully trust in You, help is on the way.
I jump for joy and burst forth with ecstatic, passionate praise!
I will sing songs of what You mean to me!"
Psalm 28:7 TPT (The Passion Translation) (emphasis added)
"Let everyone give all their praise and thanks to the Lord!
Here's why—He's better than anyone could ever imagine.
Yes, He's always loving and kind, and His faithful love never ends."
Psalm 107:1 TPT (The Passion Translation) (emphasis added)

There are many scriptures and reference books available to encourage a daily attitude of gratitude. I encourage you to think about things you are thankful for, write them down, and speak of them in prayer. As you sow gratefulness, you will reap a harvest of blessings.

"And in the midst of everything be always giving thanks,
for this is God's perfect plan for you in Christ Jesus."
1 Thessalonians 5:18 TPT (The Passion Translation)

12

DID YOU COME TO JESUS?

his is such an important question! As you read my journey, please think about your relationship with Jesus.

Before I share the details about the most important defining moment in my life with you, let me provide a bit of backstory leading up to it.

I wonder if any readers can identify with what I'm saying here. Since childhood, I've experienced periods where I feel as though part of me is like a kite, up in the clouds, being pulled along with a thin string. And, whenever threatened or scared during rough periods of my life, I can pop back into the clouds easily. I believe it began while I experienced child abuse with a form of dissociation, where the Lord enabled me to bear physical and emotional pain that I otherwise would not have endured. The Lord is always in control, but in those incidents, He was truly at the helm for my benefit.

I married my high-school sweetheart shortly after graduation, something almost every couple in my graduating class had done. Since our class reunion is this year, I'm surprised to realize it was fifty years ago.

He and I had lots of passion and emotions going on, maybe even hatred and anger. We both came from broken homes; we had no idea how to make a happy home. After being married a year, I had my son; approximately three years later I was four-months pregnant on that momentous day.

Sunday morning, February 9, 1975, began as nothing special compared to any other Sunday.

As soon as I woke up I decided, seemingly with no apparent reason or on a whim, to step out of the home by myself. To say this was unusual for me to do is an understatement. In fact, I had never simply decided to leave my son (then three years old) alone with my husband unless it was a short pre-planned trip, such as to the doctor or for groceries.

Was the Lord prompting me to go? Looking back now, I think so.

I was filled with the urge to leave my home alone, yet I didn't have any destination in mind. I dressed up, fed us all breakfast, and announced my intentions. My husband assumed I was going to church, so I decided to play that out; I grabbed my Bible as I went out the door. Once in the car, though, I couldn't decide where to go. As I drove aimlessly, it seemed nothing was open on a Sunday morning, and I could think of nothing to do. So, without a plan or idea what to do next, I decided to drive the short distance to my sister's house.

She answered the door with her hair a mess, and a robe on. To *my* surprise, I asked her, "Are you going to church?" Confused, I questioned myself, *why did you say that?*

My sister immediately said, "Yes!" and she quickly got ready to go. She was excited, saying this was the best birthday present I could give her.

I thought to myself, *"Oh yea, I forgot! She's been pestering me to go to church with her for some time, and tomorrow's her birthday."*

We went to a little country "hellfire and brimstone" church, where the preacher was extremely dramatic, with his face turning red and sweat pouring from his face as he yelled his sermon at us. He was a plump little man, and I worried he may collapse.

While songs were being sung at the end of the service, I noticed church staff were aggressively talking to those who were not singing, persuading them to come forward. Some of those in the pews being spoken to appeared confused while others were reluctant, as they allowed themselves to be led up the aisle. I certainly did not want that happening to me! I had guessed those who didn't sing were considered the "sinners." Some stood crying while others kneeled in prayer.

I determined to smile and sing vigorously, so they wouldn't drag me to the alter.

After a few songs, we began to sing "In the Garden." That song had been my mother's favorite. While we sang, my mind traveled to the past; I cried uncontrollably.

I considered the many years of my family's ugly, dysfunctional and violent past. I thought about the precious few happy memories that I had with my mother, who I had loved desperately. I remembered horrible scenes of experienced child abuse. My mother had died under suspicious circumstances while I was a teenager.

Still crying, I suddenly felt as if I was no longer alone in my thoughts. Others, unseen, were around me, one on my left, and another on my right. They were whispering in my ears. Was it some kind of a spiritual encounter? They were fighting for my soul!

One of them reminded me of how religiously mixed up and "out of balance" my parents had been, as they had fought venomously over Baptist beliefs versus those of my father's cult.

I agreed, I sure didn't want to be anything like them! Nope, religion is not for me!

The other asked, "Does it make sense to refuse the only way, the truth and the life? To give up eternity because of the choices other people (my parents) had made?"

My answer was clear, "No, I have known the salvation message from childhood. I know Jesus is my only hope."

Then the first voice whispered, "What God would allow the pain and suffering of innocent children? Where was God when you were beaten? Where was He when your baby brother was seriously crippled?"

Then I heard Jesus, "I was with you through it all! And I'm with you now! I will never leave you! Suffering on earth is only for a moment compared to the joy of everlasting life with me!"

I knew this to be true, I knew it with all my heart!

To stop the arguments, and to declare my personal decision through action, I jumped into the aisle and quickly marched up to the altar. There, I asked for forgiveness of my sins, all of them, and I accepted Jesus as my Lord and Savior.

In that instance, my life was FOREVER CHANGED! I *knew* in that instant, I had become a new creature in Jesus Christ; I was saved, born-again!

The next Sunday I was baptized. I wanted everyone to know how Jesus saved me and changed my life. I was baptized by water immersion to demonstrate my death with Jesus to the old life, and the resurrected life with Jesus, into my new life as His believer.

Following the baptism, I changed into dry clothing and joined the congregation. There, I felt the Lord hug me and whisper in my ear, "I remembered you..."

I immediately flashed back to those days during my teens that we spent on Grandma's farm. I loved to play the old record player, dancing and singing (making fun of) the old gospel song, "Do LORD, Do LORD, Do Remember Me..." Yes, my Heavenly Father surely did remember me; in fact, He never gave up on me!

I had begun the process of my Christian walk. That same year, I was blessed with the birth of my daughter.

I was intensely focused on the Lord for several years and enjoyed inner peace and joy; but over time, I began to allow life's distractions to affect me. I allowed my focus to waver.

My knight in shining armor soon rescued me following the emotional and financial destruction of a failed marriage, but I remained a Baby Christian. After seven years in a secure and loving home, His passing brought me to a period of depression...You may recall that I've already told you about my Fall while in my early forties when I had failed at another relationship and turned my back on the Lord.

After pulling away from the Lord and from His protection, I found myself in a relationship with a dangerous and evil man who abused me. He even tried to take my life. When I could no longer bear the pain of despair and torture, I humbly cried out to the Lord.

What did I seek from the Lord? Forgiveness, rescue, and salvation.

I had desperately needed forgiveness for my sinful living, for all of my failings as a daughter, mother, sister, and friend; especially, I needed forgiveness for turning my back on the Lord, after all He had done for me.

Why did He forgive me? God *is* love, He is merciful, and He saw my heart to be contrite and humble. He forgave me; He gave me a way to escape that situation. He responded as in Psalm 40:1-3, lifting me out of the miry pit and giving me a new song to sing.

As you know, my recovery was long. Seven years ago, I rededicated my life to the Lord. He had never left me from the day I had accepted Jesus as my Lord and Savior in 1975, but I had remained a Baby Christian, sometimes not at all appearing to be a Child of God. What an unfailing, patient God we have!

We can turn to God for help, run to Him with urgency! He is aware of all our evil thoughts, ugly words, and actions, even those in the past and future, and He still loves us. He waits for us to turn to Him.

In the previous chapter, we discussed sowing and reaping as we make choices. Here are words of wisdom:

> "If you cover up your sin you'll never do well.
> But if you confess your sins and forsake them,
>   you will be kissed by mercy."
> Proverbs 28:13 TPT (The Passion Translation)

The Bible has much to say about choices. We can choose death, evilness, and chaos; or we can choose life, goodness, and peace. We decide! We can't do anything about the past, but we can repent of it and forsake our sinful living, and walk into the present with a changed mindset for a good future.

> "For the Scriptures say, 'If you want to enjoy life
> and see many happy days,
> keep your tongue from speaking evil and your lips from telling lies.
> Turn away from evil and do good. Search for peace,
> and work to maintain it.
> The eyes of the LORD watch over those who do right,
> and His ears are open to their prayers.
> But the LORD turns his face against those who do evil.'"
> 1 Peter 3:10-12 NLT (New Living Translation) (emphasis added)

If you are not yet a believer, you can humbly turn to our Creator while you have opportunity; pray, repent, and walk away from that sinful life; accept Jesus as your Lord and Savior.

Going forward, you can find great counsel through the Word of God, through the great Counselor, the Holy Spirit; you can find fellow believers in a good Bible-based church and enjoy strength in unity among believers.

We have evidence of our Heavenly Father's unconditional love for us in the Word of God as in John 3:16, and we can see His love in the daily mercies He brings to us, although none of us deserve it.

> "But God demonstrates His own love for us in this:
> While we were still sinners, Christ died for us."
> Romans 5:8 NIV (New International Version) (emphasis added)

> "My dear children, I write this to you so that you will not sin.
> But if anybody does sin,
> we have an advocate with the Father—
> Jesus Christ, the Righteous One.
> He is the atoning sacrifice for our sins, and not only for ours but
> also for the sins of the whole world."
> 1 John 2:1-2 NIV (New International Version)

Our Creator sacrificed His only Son for us, allowing Jesus Christ to be crucified on the cross to pay for our sins, and Jesus defeated death. Our part is by free choice if we will repent and walk away from our sins and accept Jesus.

Do you know the way? Yes. Jesus himself said it clearly, in John 14:6; see also Acts 2:21, 4:11-12 and other scriptures.

"'… Believe in the Lord Jesus, and you will be saved…'"
Acts 16:31 NIV (New International Version)

If you believe, this is the opportunity to tell Him. It's your personal decision to make.

[11] and every tongue acknowledge that Jesus Christ is Lord,
to the glory of God the Father.
Philippians 2:11 NIV (New International Version)

Regardless where you may stand today in your relationship with the Lord, I sincerely urge you to please pray this version of what is often called the "Sinner's Prayer" (with basic elements that come from the Word of God) now, with a humble and contrite heart, confessing to Jesus out loud:

"Dear Lord Jesus,
I know that You are the only begotten Son of God.
I know that You suffered on the cross for me. for my sins.
And I believe that You defeated death.
You arose from the grave on the third day.

But, I'm a sinner! I ask You to forgive me.
I repent of my sins. I walk away from them now.
Please help me stand firm, because I know I will be tempted.

I need You, Jesus!
I am nothing, I am hopeless without You.

I ask You, Jesus, to come into my heart and
to be my Lord and Savior.
And I will serve You all of my life!
In Jesus Name,
Amen."

With this prayer, you are telling the Lord that you believe. You are sincerely choosing to walk away from a sinful life, and He will help you in doing that. You are also pledging to serve Him. In all of this, you have decided to begin a relationship with Jesus. You are saved, redeemed, born-again. The Holy Spirit now resides in you, guiding and comforting you. The Holy Spirit intercedes as you pray to the Father, even when you're not sure how to pray. He equips you with the Fruit of the Spirit (Galatians 5:22-23), and you are never forsaken, never alone.

Your Christian walk, which is also referred to as the process of "working out your own salvation," is your journey. It may take some time as you travel from a Baby Christian through various distractions and challenges toward growth into your maturity. I have shared with you my walk, which was riddled with overwhelming circumstances and horrible mistakes. I pray that you learn lessons from my experiences so that you won't follow such a rough pathway. I ask you to seriously consider the Apostle Paul's motivation:

"Therefore, my dear friends, as you have always obeyed—not only
in my presence, but now much more in my absence—continue to
work out your salvation with fear and trembling,
for it is God who works in you to will and to act in order
to fulfill His good purpose."
Philippians 2:12-13 NIV (New International Version)
(emphasis added)

I encourage you to study the Word of God and pray. As you do this, you can gain an understanding of who He is and learn of the many promises He offers. Regardless of your circumstances, always praise and obey the Lord with gratitude as you grow in faith. In all of this, you are developing a deeper relationship with Jesus; your character is becoming more and more like Jesus. Again, here is more inspiration from the Apostle Paul to believers:

"Look at how much encouragement you've found in your
relationship with the Anointed One! You are filled to overflowing
with His comforting love.
You have experienced a deepening friendship
with the Holy Spirit and
have felt His tender affection and mercy.
So I'm asking you, my friends, that you be
joined together in perfect unity—
with one heart, one passion, and united in one love.
Walk together with one harmonious purpose and you will fill my
heart with unbounded joy."
Philippians 2:1-2 TPT (The Passion Translation)

When you follow Jesus, you are the light of the world! The Holy Spirit within you will motivate you to encourage and help others, so your light will shine.

"'You are the light of the world.
A town built on a hill cannot be hidden.
Neither do people light a lamp and put it under a bowl.
Instead they put it on its stand, and
it gives light to everyone in the house.
In the same way, let your light shine before others, that they may see
your good deeds and glorify your Father in heaven.'"
Matthew 5:14-16 NIV (New International Version)

13

CAN YOU RUN THE RACE?

*I*s there something that you keep in your heart and mind, maybe a dream, talent, or goal, that you believe you should be doing in life? Do you know what your purpose in life is? Are you asking God about it?

Have you been discouraged from taking that first step toward your dream? Maybe you have approached it, but circumstances or people got in the way. Now you might be taking a break to rest and rethink what your dream, mission, or goal was really about, and when or how it should be executed. Does fear enter into your thinking?

Does it matter if you lack the faith to do what you have been created to do? Isn't that lack of faith not only in yourself but in what the Lord can accomplish through you? Here is God's response to a lack of faith in Him:

"'When I came to you, why was no one there?
When I called, why did no one answer?
Am I powerless to rescue you or too weak to deliver you?
With only a threat I can evaporate the sea and
dry up the rivers as a desert,

leaving the fish to rot and die of thirst.'"
Isaiah 50:2 TPT (The Passion Translation)

But, what if instead of giving in to worry and fear, you choose to turn in faith to depend on the Lord for help in what needs to be accomplished?

"But those who wait for Yahweh's *grace*
will experience *divine* strength.
They will rise up on soaring wings and fly like eagles,
run *their race* without growing weary,
and walk *through life* without giving up."
Isaiah 40:31 TPT (The Passion Translation)

Please note that the name Yahweh is the Hebrew name for God, our Creator.

The Lord prepares us. We need to evaluate our goal and ensure that what we seek to do is based upon a solid foundation. Let me remind you of two things our Heavenly Father tells us:

- Jeremiah 1:5 - "Before I formed you in the womb I knew you."
- Jeremiah 29:11 - "'For I know the thoughts that I think toward you,' says the Lord, 'thoughts of peace and not of evil, to give you a future and a hope.'"

God had a plan for your life even from before you were born. It may not seem like it now, but He has great things in store for you. But you will face conflicts amid spiritual warfare for your soul (Ephesians 6). The enemy, the thief, wants to steal, kill, and to destroy you. Jesus wants you to have life, and to have it abundantly (John 10:10).

The enemy certainly does not want you to accomplish anything that God has designed you for. The enemy does not want you to fulfill your purpose in life. If there is a way he can do it, the enemy will derail you. Spiritual warfare can happen when you least expect it, and it can distract you from your objectives.

What if distractions in life have brought your energy level to an all-time low, and you feel reluctant to put forth the effort to begin or continue a project that you initially felt the Lord had laid on your heart? With the COVID-19 Pandemic, for instance, maybe being unable to continue your normal routine brought you into a sluggish or lazy mode? Maybe you gave up on it, saying to yourself, "What's the use?" Just as easily you can determine:

> "But me, I'm not giving up. I'm sticking around to
> see what GOD will do.
> I'm waiting for God to make things right.
> I'm counting on God to listen to me.
> Don't, enemy, crow over me. I'm down, but I'm not out.
> I'm sitting in the dark right now, but GOD is my light."
> Micah 7:7-8 MSG (The Message)

To remain in a state of sluggishness or laziness brings us to the sin of sloth that we touched on in a previous chapter, "Does Sin Apply To You?" Again, the enemy has attacked, tempting a person to be lax or to let go of the opportunity to thrive in their calling. With genuine efforts of others to help us in a time of need, we can be tempted even in our receipt of help. For instance, it is unfortunate, but even with efforts to help others during the Pandemic, there have been occasions when laborers received stimulus checks. Once they had that money in their hand, they did not return to work.

Does it matter if you have become lazy? There are many scriptures that reference this topic, especially in Proverbs. Here, King Solomon shares practical wisdom:

> "Laziness leads to a sagging roof; idleness leads to a leaky house."
> Ecclesiastes 10:18 NLT (New Living Translation)
> "Plant your seed in the morning and keep busy all afternoon, for
> you don't know

if profit will come from one activity or another—or maybe both."
Ecclesiastes 11:6 NLT (New Living Translation)

Maybe you have lost your enthusiasm because of things happening around you, and the zeal you once had in what you felt as your God-given goal, is now an attitude of indifference. You have become "lukewarm." Is there any harm in that? What if that same change in attitude applied to someone you loved, maybe a fiancé? Would it then matter if their interest level in you became apathetic or indifferent? Of course! This scripture relating to a Christian's lack of commitment may startle you:

"'I know all the things you do, that you are neither hot nor cold.
I wish that you were one or the other!
But since you are like lukewarm water, neither hot nor cold,
I will spit you out of my mouth!'"
Revelation 3:15-16 NLT (New Living Translation)

Whew! How many of us are now taking a serious look at our level of enthusiasm as we follow our dreams? Or as we serve the Lord? All of us?

Please remember the cloak of zeal as part of your armor against the enemy (Isaiah 59:17). You are saved by the grace of God through Jesus, not of your own works; so out of gratitude you are motivated to do good works zealously.

"Put your heart and soul into every activity you do,
as though you are doing it for the Lord himself
and not merely for others.
For we know that we will receive a reward,
an inheritance from the Lord,
as we serve the Lord Yahweh, the Anointed One!"
Colossians 3:23-24 TPT (The Passion Translation)

For some of you, after enduring domestic violence or other very dark circumstances or situations, you may picture it as impossible to realize anything better. But God never wanted you to suffer oppression and abuse. Please remember, what the enemy has meant for your harm, God will make for your good, so you can fulfill the unique purpose He put in you.

> "But blessed is the one who trusts in the LORD,
>   whose confidence is in Him.
> They will be like a tree planted by the water that
>   sends out its roots by the stream.
> It does not fear when heat comes; its leaves are always green.
> It has no worries in a year of drought and never fails to bear fruit."

You might have walked out of a toxic environment of mean-spirited people. But maybe you still feel unworthy, or afraid. You can decide to trust in the Lord in Jeremiah 17 (above) and have faith that you have fruit to bear (a calling). You can decide to be brave, like Deborah in Judges 5, or Queen Esther in the book of Esther, or Daniel in the lion's den in Daniel 6. The Bible shares about the bravery of many men and women of God who you can emulate. In every instance, the focus was upon the Lord and His Kingdom, and not upon themselves or their circumstances.

You may remember the story told in Daniel 3, about three brave young men of faith, Shadrach, Meshach, and Abednego. King Nebuchadnezzar had made an image of gold, an idol. Everyone was to fall down and worship this idol or be thrown into a burning fiery furnace. But Shadrach, Meshach, and Abednego refused to do this.

They decided to serve the living God, regardless of the circumstances. The King went into an angry rage. Still, he gave them another opportunity to fall down and worship his idol.

> "If we are thrown into the blazing furnace,
>   the God whom we serve is able to save us.
> He will rescue us from your power, Your Majesty.
> But even if He doesn't, we want to make it clear to you,

Your Majesty, that we will never serve your gods or worship the
gold statue you have set up."'
Daniel 3:17-18 NLT (New Living Translation) (emphasis added)

In other translations, verse 18 says, "but if not..." These courageously faithful men were willing to lose their lives if that was God's
will. Regardless of the threats, they were not willing to disobey
God's commandments. They were thrown into the furnace after it
was made even hotter than before, and these men were tied up.
Even the men who threw them in were burned. But when the King
and others looked in, they saw a fourth person walking inside the
furnace with them, who had the form like the Son of God. These
brave men were delivered from harm. In verse 28, King Nebuchadnezzar praised and blessed the God of Shadrach, Meshach, and
Abednego.

Many years later, found in the New Testament, the Apostle Paul
prayed, knowing God could remove his weakness (also referred to
as a thorn or his light affliction). But if not, Paul vowed to continue
to follow and worship the Lord in ministry. Paul's affliction was not
removed, and he learned to be content whether he was living in
good conditions or not.

"For our light and momentary troubles are achieving for us an
eternal glory that far outweighs them all. So we fix our eyes not on
what is seen, but on what is unseen,
since what is seen is temporary, but what is unseen is eternal."
2 Corinthians 4:17-18 NIV (New International Version)

Have you ever had the opportunity to take a stand for God and
His commandments, regardless of the circumstances? Maybe you
said something like these men did, "My God will help me in this
situation, *but if not*, I will still praise Him!" Maybe it wasn't with a
threat to your life, but with your resolve in the situation, you were
able to influence another person to turn to God. How awesome to
have your faithful courage working for an Eternal harvest.

Pressing on in the specific purpose we have is the race we run. It may include being the best artist we can be, the best business administrator, or performing good works within a ministry that points to the glory of God. I believe that all followers of Jesus, whether they have a separate purpose in life or not, they are called to serve the Lord.

In all of whatever we do, we can take a stand for the Lord and His commandments. We can run that race with unfailing faith in God, even when heartbreaking losses happen. We can be obedient while mourning, while not understanding why things happened the way they do. We can press on with self-discipline, as described in 1 Corinthians 9:24-27.

I began writing this book early into 2020, and then the Pandemic hit with its own complications. My heart was broken when my son suddenly died in his sleep, just before Mother's Day. Challenges happen while we run our race *and* God is our strength and refuge through it all. I remember and remind you how the Lord was with Joseph in the midst of his challenges (when he was sold into slavery by his brothers (Gen. 37:12-36), falsely accused by Potiphar's wife (Gen. 39:13-18), and imprisoned for years (Gen. 39:20). Yet, Joseph remained faithful and not bitter; the Lord worked it all out for good.

When I look at the life of Joseph and so many others, I have confidence that as my challenges come, the Lord will continue to strengthen my resolve to complete the work I began. As I do this, I can hope for good results.

Before my son's death, I had continually prayed for his health and welfare; I heard his testimony of salvation. Therefore, knowing God's will and timing is always perfect, and that God is love and good--in that faith, I praise and lean on the Lord through my mourning. I am receiving inner peace and joy that only comes from the Lord.

We need to decide to follow and serve our Creator and depend upon Him for the end results. What the Lord said to Joshua, is true for us today:

"'Have I not commanded you? Be strong and courageous.
Do not be afraid; do not be discouraged,
for the LORD your God will be with you wherever you go.'"
Joshua 1:9 NIV (New International Version)

Have you found your calling to be within the ministry? As believers, we "walk in light," as in Ephesians 5, representing Jesus as light and as His hands and feet. In 2 Corinthians 5:17-21, those who share the good news of Jesus Christ act as His ambassadors.

"So we are Christ's ambassadors;
God is making his appeal through us.
We speak for Christ when we plead, 'Come back to God!'"
2 Corinthians 5:20 NLT (New Living Translation)

Within the ministry, and as believers generally, we all should ever be conscious that the name of Jesus is powerful. In Acts 3 is an account of a man who had been lame for forty years; he was healed in the name of Jesus Christ by the Apostle Peter. In Acts 4, the priests and captain of the temple guard and the Sadducees were upset that healing was performed in the name of Jesus. Peter, filled with the Holy Spirit, declared:

"'... then know this, you and all the people of Israel: It is by the name of Jesus Christ of Nazareth, whom you crucified but whom God raised from the dead, that this man stands before you healed. Jesus is "the stone you builders rejected,
which has become the cornerstone."
Salvation is found in no one else,
for there is no other name under heaven
given to mankind by which we must be saved.'"
Acts 4:10-12 NIV (New International Version)

Do you know what His plan for your life is? Whether it is to be a full-time mother, a musician, or in an aspect of the ministry, do you believe God will equip you to accomplish your purpose in life? What will it take?

Ask, and God will give you dreams, goals, and your unique purpose. Believe, have faith, and decide to act upon it before it all becomes a reality. Prayerfully listen for God's voice as He sets your path before you, then be active in your faith, one step at a time.

There are other believers around you who are supportive and like-minded; they can join you in your quest. Please know, with God, all things are possible. He can make things happen in your life using many resources and formats that you cannot even imagine. He is not limited on what can be accomplished. In all of it, remain enthusiastic, consistent, and bold.

We can do all things which God has called us to do because we have Jesus empowering us to fulfill His purpose for us (Philippians 4:13). As we faithfully believe, Jesus provides us with the inner strength and confident peace we need.

I have an affirmation card taped to the mirror in my bathroom so I will see it early and often daily. Within the card is a picture of a woman running to the finish line in a race. It is a constant reminder! The words on my card are these, "I am courageous and bold to run the race set before me, regardless of the obstacles." On another side of the same card, "I am well equipped to achieve my goals that God has called me to do!"

Where did I get this inspiration? From the Word of God, which is the Sword of the Spirit. I encourage you to daily draw your weapon by studying His Word. Affirmations for specific areas of need can be made by declaring applicable scriptures.

The Apostle Paul encouraged the Philippians by using himself as an example, and he now inspires us as well:

"No, dear brothers and sisters, I have not achieved it,
but I focus on this one thing:
Forgetting the past and looking forward to what lies ahead,
I press on to reach the end of the race and
receive the heavenly prize for which God,

through Christ Jesus, is calling us."
Philippians 3:13-14 NLT (New Living Translation)

When the Lord prompts you with your specific calling, will you say "Yes," and begin your journey, one step of faith at a time?

When in your race, will you give it your all?

Do you anticipate there will be periods that the race requires courage and hard work, but you have decided to press on?

Are you determined to maintain your hope and prayerful, patient faith through to the end, knowing that you are not alone in it?

14

EPILOGUE

This could be your story of how the Lord delivered you from the challenges or storms of life you have faced:

"Some of us set sail upon the sea to faraway ports,
transporting our goods from ship to shore.
We were witnesses of God's power out in the ocean deep;
we saw breathtaking wonders upon the high seas.
When God spoke He stirred up a storm,
lifting high the waves with hurricane winds.
Ships were tossed by swelling sea, rising to the sky,
then dropping down to the depths,
reeling like drunkards, spinning like tops,
everyone at their wits' end until even sailors despaired of life,
cringing in terror.
Then we cried out, "Lord, help us! Rescue us!" And He did!
God stilled the storm, calmed the waves, and
He hushed the hurricane winds to only a whisper.
We were so relieved, so glad as
He guided us safely to harbor in a quiet haven.
So lift your hands and give thanks to God

for His marvelous kindness
and for His miracles of mercy for those He loves!
Let's exalt Him on high and lift up our praises in public;
let all the people and the leaders of the nation know
how great and wonderful is Yahweh, our God!"
Psalm 107:23-32 TPT (The Passion Translation) (emphasis added)

My overall purpose in writing to you, my dear readers, is to offer encouragement as you face your hardships. I especially write to women who have suffered from domestic violence and other abuses, and to offer all of you a recipe for overcoming based upon my journey.

As I shared my testimony of how the Lord repeatedly rescued me through traumatic periods, I believe I offered real-life proof that the Lord is loving and merciful. We can learn from those horrible storms in our lives, grow stronger, and help others along the way. Always, we can rest assured that what the enemy means for evil, God always has a plan for good.

Let's review. What is it that you can do, what actions can you take, in every instance when you face various enemy attacks from every side?

Turn to God

Turn to God, your Creator, who is able to help you in any situation. Turn to Him for forgiveness, rescue, and salvation. Does He love you enough to do it?

Didn't He sacrifice His only Son, to come to earth and suffer, even to the point of death to pay for your sins? And Jesus arose! When you accept Jesus, you have permanently joined the winning side. The enemy strives to destroy you, but nothing can separate you from His love, and Jesus has already overcome. Lean on Him, cast your cares, and He will fight your battles in amazing ways.

In the world today, wickedness shouts out: "It's not your fault, you were born this way; you don't need God, you don't need to repent or give up your sinful ways. You aren't held responsible for what you've done or what you're doing." The world works to convince us the opposite of God's moral compass, that what is good is bad, and what is bad is good.

For example, let's imagine a criminal, a habitual offender, was caught and found guilty of multiple assaults, leading to homicide. He says, "I was born this way," giving excuses for his evil ways, blaming it on others, his victims, and even giving blame to his Creator.

That criminal was born into sin, as each of us are, which can be traced back to the fall of Adam and Eve. With that, he may have had the propensity in him to follow after evil and to commit crimes. But it is with our own decisions, whether we choose good, which brings life or evil that clings to death. In Deuteronomy 30:19-20, we are encouraged to choose life.

"Surely I was sinful at birth,
sinful from the time my mother conceived me."
Psalm 51:5 NIV (New International Version)
"… for all have sinned and fall short of the glory of God,"
Romans 3:23 NIV (New International Version)
"If we claim to be without sin, we deceive ourselves
and the truth is not in us.
If we confess our sins, He is faithful and just
and will forgive us our sins and purify us
from all unrighteousness. If we claim we have not sinned,
we make Him out to be a liar and His word is not in us."
1 John 1:8-10 NIV (New International Version) (emphasis added)

That habitual criminal had free will to decide whether he would chase after good or evil. At any point, he could have changed his mindset, and begun a new way to follow. This is true for each person. Everyone is born with free will to decide the path they will take.

"When tempted, no one should say, 'God is tempting me.' For God cannot be tempted by evil, nor does He tempt anyone; but each person is tempted when they are dragged away by their own evil desire and enticed. Then, after desire has conceived,
it gives birth to sin;
and sin, when it is full-grown, gives birth to death."
James 1:13-15 NIV (New International Version) (emphasis added)
"If anyone, then, knows the good they ought to do and doesn't do it,
it is sin for them."
James 4:17 NIV (New International Version)

Assuming this habitual criminal remains unrepentant when he faces God, he must answer for every thought and action he has done. Will the wicked philosophers who shouted immorality as good be with that criminal for defense? No, he will face God alone. Will excuses bring him a pass for evil ways? No. This is important; do not be misled! Every person will be held accountable for their own decisions, whether they were good or evil choices made. Your only hope and my only hope is in Jesus *while* opportunity knocks.

As in Acts 10, the Apostle Peter was led by God to proclaim this message: Anyone who believes in Jesus, that He is the Son of God who was crucified as payment for our sins and raised from the dead in three days, repents of their sins and accepts Jesus as their Lord and Savior *is* a child of God. They are saved through the blood of Jesus Christ, receiving God's grace and mercy, and belong to the Kingdom of God.

As a believer, when we face the Lord's judgment, we have the blood of Jesus covering our sins because He has already paid the price.

"But God demonstrates His own love for us in this:
While we were still sinners, Christ died for us.
⁹ Since we have now been justified by His blood, how much more shall we be saved from God's wrath through Him!"
Romans 5:8-9 NIV (New International Version)

"If you declare with your mouth, 'Jesus is Lord,' and believe in your
heart that God raised him from the dead, you will be saved. For it is
with your heart that you believe and are justified, and
it is with your mouth that you profess your faith and are saved."
Romans 10:9-10 NIV (New International Version)

SAFELY LEAVE YOUR DANGEROUS ENVIRONMENT

Are you in the company of habitually toxic and mean-spirited
people? I encourage you to prayerfully decide to remove yourself
from the enemy's camp, but that can be a dangerous move to make.
Call upon the Lord to deliver you, *and* seek professional help:

CALL "911" IF YOU'RE IN AN EMERGENCY SITUATION.

Call your local shelter or call the National Domestic Violence
Hotline Number for assistance in your escape plan, and to help
arrange your physical shelter:

1-800-799-7233 (SAFE)

Regardless of whether you are a believer or not, spiritual warfare is
happening all around you. The enemy whispers evil thoughts and
uses people and circumstances; temptations are being thrust at you
constantly. Is there an escape? Are you well equipped? Can you put
on the full armor of God? My next book, *Stand With Your Armor On*,
addresses everyday life situations where it makes a difference what
choices we make and if we are wearing our armor or not.

"No temptation has overtaken you
except what is common to mankind.
And God is faithful; He will not let you be tempted
beyond what you can bear.
But when you are tempted, He will also provide a way out

so that you can endure it."
1 Corinthians 10:13 NIV (New International Version)
(emphasis added)

Believe and Have Faith

You may have begun your journey believing yourself as nothing or unworthy. For a time, you may have remained under your adversary's feet. Was there fear involved? Did you turn to the Lord? Do you belong to Jesus?

The Lord created every living thing; He is certainly able to handle your problems, your battles. Give them all to God and move on. Chose this day whether you will remain filled with fear or you will be filled with faith.

What does the Word of God say about you? Who are you in Christ Jesus? How tremendous is the power of God to His believers! Ultimate victory is found in Jesus!

"I pray that you will continually experience
the immeasurable greatness of God's power
made available to you through faith. Then your lives will be an
advertisement of this immense power as it works through you!
This is the mighty power that was released when God raised Christ
from the dead and exalted him to the place of highest honor and
supreme authority in the heavenly realm!"
Ephesians 1:19-20 TPT (The Passion Translation)

Will you be considered "less than" or slighted in heaven? No!

"For God does not show favoritism."
Romans 2:11 NIV (New International Version)

God tells us how much He loves us:

"I have loved you with an everlasting love;
I have drawn you with unfailing kindness,
I will build you up ... you will take up your timbrels
and go out to dance with the joyful."
Jeremiah 31:3-4 NIV (New International Version)

We can hope in the Lord and soar like eagles; we may grow weary but not faint. Please look up scriptures and use them as references in times when they are needed, to build your affirmation as to who you are in Jesus Christ. Here are some to get you started: Jeremiah 31:3; 1 Corinthians 2:16, 3:9-16, 6:17-20; Philippians 1:6, 3:20, 4:13-19; Colossians 1:22, 2:7-10, 3:12; Hebrews 4:16... and, here are a few examples:

I AM THE LORD'S WORKMANSHIP, HIS WORK OF ART

"For we are His workmanship,
created in Christ Jesus for good works,
which God prepared beforehand that we should walk in them."
Ephesians 2:10 NKJV (New King James Version)

I Am a Loved Child of God

"But as many as received Him,
to them He gave the right to become children of God,
to those who believe in His name..."
John 1:12 NKJV (New King James Version)
"We have come into an intimate experience with God's love, and
we trust in the love He has for us.
God is love!
Those who are living in love are living in God,
and God lives through them."
1 John 4:16 TPT (The Passion Translation)

Be Filled with Gratitude

Let me reiterate, we cannot have a thankful attitude at the same time that we wallow in a pity-party; they are opposites. We cannot truly be grateful *and* be filled with self-pity at the same time. It's not possible. The Lord commands us to rejoice always (Philippians 4:4), and for everything that has breath to praise the Lord (Psalm 150:6). Is it an important matter? Oh, yes!

Please indulge me to share a story relating to something said by my son one day. It remains a constant reminder for me to be thankful. Maybe it will affect you as well.

Several years ago, while my son worked as a laborer at a construction site, and I worked a desk job for the Commonwealth of Virginia, we had a short phone call that evening. I had experienced a particularly stressful, chaotic day. As he and I talked, I whined and complained while he patiently listened. Once I was finished, he asked (rather sarcastic in tone), "Oh, did you have to run a jackhammer in the sun all day, without a lunch?" That shut me up.

Can you picture it?

Whatever we may go through, there is always someone else who has more to deal with. We can be thankful for the condition we're in; we can pray for those who have more hardships to face. With our gratitude, we are motivated to bless others, sowing good into their lives; and as we bless others, we reap a harvest of blessings.

"Beloved ones, God has called us to live a life of freedom
in the Holy Spirit.
But don't view this wonderful freedom as an opportunity to set up a
base of operations in the natural realm. Freedom means that
we become so completely free of self-indulgence
that we become servants of one another,
expressing love in all we do."
Galatians 5:13 TPT (The Passion Translation)

FORGIVE YOURSELF, THOSE WHO ABUSED OR OFFENDED YOU, AND THE INDIFFERENT

Have you asked for God's forgiveness? Have you forgiven everyone, including yourself? This is a very hard step, one that you may have found must be done repeatedly. But you do it for your own peace, and so that the Lord will also forgive you.

From the time I began writing this book to you, I have felt especially close to the Lord, knowing that He is guiding me. However, I am not free of enemy attacks. During the process of writing this last chapter, I suffered enemy attacks. Here, they were not physical attacks but brought suffering nonetheless. I share with you so that you can understand there are real examples of how the enemy comes after us.

One pleasant evening, I overheard a small part of a conversation and assumed I knew the rest. Instantly, I recalled an offense from the past, and I felt pain as if the offense was happening again. Anger was triggered! Not immediately, and not before saying a few ugly words, I cried out to Jesus and began leaning on Him. I prayed about it, forgiving people of the past all over again. I asked forgiveness for my freshly lit upset and bitterness. I acknowledged, what happens on earth is temporary, and regained focus on His Kingdom. To "seal the deal," I read Psalm 30 through 40, all ten chapters, out loud. My mind, my heart was then at peace.

Looking at that incident, I must wonder, was there residual unforgiveness that I had buried inside? How many times must I forgive? Seventy times seven? As much as it takes!

Once we have traveled past a hard spot, are we then immune to further trials to happen? What do you think? I believe we need to remain alert and stay ready!

On May 25, 2020, a startling and malicious crime was committed. I and many others, watched the violence unfold on video. Four white Minneapolis police officers arrested George Floyd, a black man. While Floyd remained handcuffed, one of the officers decided to put his knee into Floyd's neck, steadily applying pressure to cut off his air supply. This continued for several minutes, despite Floyd's desperate plea to breathe. That officer watched Floyd slowly die. While I watched this video, my ears began to ring loudly, and I thought my mind would explode. Never before had I heard of (or witnessed, with this video) another person committing murder in the same way that my abuser had hoped to kill me. I was shocked and enraged, re-living my own desperation all over again. I remembered my abuser's Satanic glee as he applied that deadly pressure on my throat while watching my breath cease. Only by the grace of God am I now alive. Thank you, Jesus!

I prayed for the Lord's compassion and peace to overwhelm George Floyd's family, friends, and the community. I again forgave my abuser and prayed for the Lord's forgiveness.

I looked to King David (who was a man after God's own heart) for how he prayed in Psalms when his enemies chased after him for his life. I prayed boldly, knowing God hears me. I prayed for His justice (not that of mere men) to be served swiftly so that all of us will see what God will do. We will all tremble in fear (reverential fear, awe, and respect) of the unlimited power and justice of our Almighty God.

We need to always be prepared, wearing the full armor of God. When the devil attacks, we need to have the Word of God (our weapon) drawn, and the shield of faith up, as we cry out to Jesus! Beware of the devil's many tricks and methods! The following prayer is like what I now pray, which is similar to something King David might've said (with his enemy in pursuit).

Dear Heavenly Father,
You are the King of the Universe,
You are the Creator of all Living things;
we know that You love Your children profoundly.
Nothing happens that You are not aware of,
nothing happens that You have no control over.
We ask You, Almighty God, to open our eyes!

Show us our wrong-doing; give each of us the Gift of Conviction.
Show us our wickedness until we repent. Lord, have mercy on us!
Dear Father, we ask You to cause a great revival;
not only in our country but in the world.
Bring change to each person.
Oh Lord, we see that there is evil all around us;
We ask You to cause the enemy's fiery darts, flaming arrows, and
<u>all</u> of the enemy's attacks to fall upon themselves,
and not upon Your children.
Cause our enemies to be completely exposed, so they are as nothing.
Heal and protect Your children, Lord;
heal and protect Your children!
Rescue us from harm's way; nothing is too great for you to handle
in Your perfect way, and in Your timing.
We believe, we know that with God all things are possible!
We praise You for all You have done in our lives, and
for all of the trials and sufferings, You have rescued us out of.
You are our strength and refuge in times of trouble.
Please forgive us of our sins and
help us to forgive those who have offended us.
Draw us away from evil temptations and
fortify our resolve to serve You.
Thank you for Your never-ending love, compassion, and mercy.
We praise and rejoice in You always for
Your grace through Jesus Christ, our Lord and Savior.
In Jesus Name
Amen

AFTERWORD

&

My Dear Reader,

What did I discover in my quest for a sense of belongingness?

That journey has been long and often frustrating because I looked to people for my validation. But as I should have known from the beginning, people are not perfect. They can and will fail me. Some will respond to temptations to harm me in various ways, and even those who are most loving and true, will eventually leave me or die.

People cannot bring me any lasting loving relationship. There will be no consistency or satisfaction in the long haul. It is all temporary at best. And, all struggles are temporary, just as my life on earth is.

But there is One with whom I can enjoy a permanent relationship, that One loves me no matter what. I can rely on Him to be with me and for me, despite what evil temptations may come with the purpose to draw my focus from Him. He is there for me through every turn in life, and so I pledge myself to the One.

Nothing can separate me from His love because that One is Jesus. I belong to the Lord.

In His name my prayer and desire is for you, dear reader, to belong to the Lord. My hope is that you will accept Jesus, become a believer, and when Jesus comes we will all unite in His Kingdom forever.

Blessings to you!
Carin

ABOUT THE AUTHOR

Carin Jayne Casey, the oldest of several children, grew up in a dysfunctional, sometimes violent home. Her family had moved from Ohio to rural West Virginia while she was a teen when tragedy struck their family. Casey married her high-school sweetheart and bore two wonderful children. Her marriage failed, and she was eventually lured into a violent and life-threatening relationship.

Casey strives to educate and encourage people to conquer life challenges. As she recovered from domestic violence, her gratitude toward the Lord motivated her to write books and to provide podcasts for others to gain tools in their overcoming process, to find victory, and enjoy life.

Casey served four years on the Board of Directors for Yeshua's House (www.yeshuashouse.net), a faith-based, non-profit safe-haven for women overcoming domestic violence and/or financial issues. She currently participates in various outreach and mission efforts with local church groups.

Casey graduated from Radford University and served the Commonwealth of Virginia for 31 years. Carin Jayne Casey is a Virginia licensed business and author's pen name.

Author. Speaker. Domestic Violence Advocate.
Ambassador for Christ.
www.CarinJayneCasey.com
www.Facebook.com/Turn2GodwCarin
CarinJayneCasey - @Turn2GodwCarin on Instagram
Subscribe to Carin Jayne Casey on YouTube

RECOMMENDED AUTHORS AND PASTORS

꒦

These are authors and pastors that I frequently enjoy. They have greatly influenced me along my path.

Lisa Bevere
Julia Cameron
Lisa Harper
David Jeremiah
Joyce Meyer
Beth Moore
Joel Osteen
Priscilla Shirer
Jonathan Stells
Andy Stanley
Charles Stanley
Raleigh Thornton

BIBLIOGRAPHY

Casey, Carin Jayne. *My Dear Rosa Jean.* Casey, 2014

    Casey, Carin Jayne. *Turn to God with Carin.,* 2016- present Podcast

NOTES

1. Prologue

1. Carin Casey, My Dear Rosa Jean 9 (Casey, 2014), back cover.
2. Carin Casey, My Dear Rosa Jean (Casey, 2014), 85.
3. Carin Casey, My Dear Rosa Jean (Casey, 2014), 155–56.

6. How Can You Heal From The Pain?

1. Carin Casey, My Dear Rosa Jean (Casey, 2014), 119.

ALSO BY CARIN JAYNE CASEY

- *My Dear Rosa Jean:* Suspense, Fiction, Christian fiction; It depicts a woman's process of overcoming domestic violence and finding victory.

- *Mystery at Candice Bay:* Mystery, Fiction, Young Adult; This is a page-turner, involving teens and their community experiencing escalating alarm as they are bombarded with unexplained events.

- *Granny Babysits the Mischievous Five:* Children's Chapter Book.

Casey continues as a podcaster since 2016 with a weekly podcast, *Turn to God with Carin* to promote overcoming challenges. All her videos are available at Carin Jayne Casey on YouTube.

CPSIA information can be obtained
at www.ICGtesting.com
Printed in the USA
LVHW040132091020
668359LV00014B/826